I wish that this book had b _____ y _____ ___ ___ real stories about adoption are such a blessing. Before my husband and I began this journey, we only knew about the adoption nightmare stores that you hear on the news. How encouraging this book would have been to us! Doris brings these stories to vivid life. It is a MUST read for anyone considering adoption or a discouraged Christian questioning God's plan. There were many times on our journey that we became discouraged and, as the book correctly reveals, adoption is not for the timid or weak of heart. But God still has miracles awaiting for you.

Joan Andrews
Director of Annual Giving
Tyler Junior College

The softer side of the abortion debate … In contrast to the front line war of words that emanate with most protest views, Doris takes us behind the scenes into real life drama. The stories contained in this book will make you smile, cry, and find a place in your heart for hurting people that are usually blurred out of the media headlines. As a Pastor, I appreciate the caring way she approaches the issues and the caring hands that she reaches out with to touch hurting hearts.

Pastor Rudy Bond
New Life Worship Center, Tyler, Texas

"Doris has gathered a treasury of hope and joy surrounding the adoption process, including Scriptural encouragement and honesty about the fears and challenges involved. This book is a testament to the hand of God with even the least of these."

Sara Maynard is a Texas attorney,
specializing in representing children.
She is Board Certified in Juvenile Law.

ADOPTION JOYS, THEY EXPECTED A MIRACLE, explains God's plan for unplanned pregnancies through moving testimonies of families who have experienced the joy of adoption. As the mother of two adopted children and one adopted grandson, I found myself rejoicing with the families through their stories. This book will be an effective tool to encourage couples to consider adopting children to complete their family. Birth parents will also understand the joy their baby will bring to the adoptive couple; and, perhaps, cause them to consider releasing their baby for adoption. God patterned adoption by adopting us into His family through His Son Jesus Çhrist. May this book challenge birth and adoptive parents to allow children to experience God's unconditional love through the gift of adoption.

Judith E. Shalllcross,
Retired Christian School principal.

ADOPTION JOYS

THEY EXPECTED A MIRACLE

Doris Howe

WestBow
PRESS
A DIVISION OF THOMAS NELSON

WestBow Press books may be ordered through booksellers or by contacting:

WestBow Press
A Division of Thomas Nelson
1663 Liberty Drive
Bloomington, IN 47403
www.westbowpress.com
1-(866) 928-1240

Because of the dynamic nature of the Internet, any web addresses or links contained in this book may have changed since publication and may no longer be valid. The views expressed in this work are solely those of the author and do not necessarily reflect the views of the publisher, and the publisher hereby disclaims any responsibility for them.

Any people depicted in stock imagery provided by Thinkstock are models, and such images are being used for illustrative purposes only.

Certain stock imagery © Thinkstock.

ISBN: 978-1-4497-1292-1 (sc)
ISBN: 978-1-4497-1291-4 (e)
ISBN: 978-1-4497-1293-8 (dj)

Library of Congress Control Number: 2011922932

All Scripture quotations, unless otherwise indicated, are taken from THE THOMPSON CHAIN-REFERENCE BIBLE NEW INTERNATIONAL VERSION © 1983 by THE B. B. KIRKBRIDGE BIBLE COMPANY, INC. and THE ZONDERVAN CORPORATION. If the quotations are shorter than one page, no permission is necessary.

Printed in the United States of America

WestBow Press rev. date: 2/28/2011

PREFACE

Adoption has been defined in the dictionary as "To take into one's family through legal means and raise as one's own child." But this definition barely scratches the surface of what all is involved in the process.

This book is designed to tell a few of the ordinary (positive and successful) stories of the common adoption miracles that happen every day. My prayer is that God will remove the fears, expose the myths, and express His incredible plan of LOVE through some of the true stories of adoption that have taken place with this one small Christian adoption agency.

There are generally three major players in the adoption "triangle". The adoptive parents choose adoption to build their families for a variety of reasons such as age or infertility. A single teen-age girl, out of love for her baby, wants more for her child than she is able to give at this time in her life. The adopted child completes the triangle. Children at times lose their parents through health failure, accidental death, or may become wards of the state when negligent parent's rights are terminated. Adoption for these children can bring security into their lives.

In reality, it is more than a triangle. Over every situation, God is there, opening hearts, directing the paths of each person involved in the process. Adoption is close to His heart, as it is a picture of how He brings us into His family.

Whatever the situation, my goal is to present the beautiful and positive side of adoption through the true stories I've encountered in the several years I've spent as a caseworker for a small Christian adoption agency. I have been a witness to how the Lord has knit families together, while at the same time ministering to the birthmother and her unique situation.

For all the couples who have walked the journey toward parenthood through adoption, their stories are basically the same. Getting off the "pill." Month after month of disappointments taking its toll. Seeing fertility doctors can bring financial drain and more disappointments. Finally, the thought of adoption began to take place. Research for the right agency was an important step in the journey. Orientations at various agencies gave encouragement and/or more disappointments. Our couples create a "life book" or family picture album, referred to as our book, for young moms to study as they choose the family who is just right to parent her child.

In the stories that follow, these couples eventually found Loving Alternative Adoption Agency. This is where their stories began to take on uniqueness and miracles.

My education, life experiences and being an adoptive mother as well, took me to this position of adoption caseworker with Loving Alternative Adoption Agency. In my time with this agency, I have helped place more than one hundred adoptions. I have walked beside and sometimes right in the middle of them. These adoption stories will cause you to laugh with some, cry with others, and generally live vicariously through their miracles, as I have done.

As an adoption caseworker, I help educate and counsel young women who find themselves in unplanned pregnancies. She will experience grief whatever her decision. Loss brings grief. Her loss can be the life she lived prior to the unplanned pregnancy. Another loss comes when the child is no longer in her arms. There are three things I can be to help her through her grief. I can be a shoulder on which she can cry, ears to listen, and arms to hold her. I am there for her.

Home studies and supervisory visits are openings for me to bond with adoptive families. These parents have shared their miracle stories. *Adoption Joys/They Expected a Miracle* is a compilation of God's involvement in those adoptions.

This book is dedicated to you, if you are an adoptive family or a prospective adoptive couple, a birth mother and/or birth family, or an adoptee. My prayer is that you will be encouraged by these personal stories as you see God's fingerprints all over each one.

LEGACY OF AN ADOPTED CHILD

Once there were two women
Who never knew each other.
One you do not remember,
The other you call mother.

Two different lives
Shaped to make yours one.
One became your guiding star,
The other became your sun.

The first gave you life,
And the second taught you to live it.
The first gave you a need for love,
And the second was there to give it.

One gave you a nationality,
The other gave you a name.
One gave you the seed of talent,
The other gave you an aim.

One gave you emotions,
The other calmed your fears.
One saw your first sweet smile,
The other dried your tears.

One gave you up,
It was all that she could do.
The other prayed for a child,
And God led her straight to you.

And now you ask me through your tears,
The age-old question through the years.

Heredity or environment—
Which are you the product of?
Neither, my darling, neither,
Just two different kinds of love.

Annonymous

MOLLIE AND OLIVIA

**"Delight yourself in the LORD and He will give you the
desires of your heart." Psalm 37:4**

**"Like a shepherd, He will care for his flock gathering the
lambs in His arms." Isaiah 40:11**

Who would ever choose adoption? There are so many risks involved.
We have all heard some horror story connected with an adoption.
Do birth families really have the right to come get the child back after
adoption? What if the birth mom had poor or no prenatal care and the
child is open to a myriad of future problems? What does "openness" in the
adoption mean? Will the birth mom show up on our door step routinely,
or randomly, to become involved with the raising of the child? What if no
birth mom likes us and we never get chosen? Is there room for compromise,
or do we just give up all control?

Each of the above fears was put to rest by the staff of a small ministry-
focused Christian agency. They were thorough, leaving nothing to chance.
Each party of the adoption triangle was as important as the other two.
Each was made to feel like he was the most important element in the
adoption journey. Learning all of this did leave us with one question.
Would a birth mother ever choose us?

We had medical proof that we would never conceive a child. Yet my
husband and I were on opposite sides of the idea of adoption. I saw it as
the only option. Duane liked our life just the two of us.

I began attending an infertility support group at church, which
was supposed to encourage me. I would learn I was not alone in my
desire to become a mommy. Month after month I returned, hearing the
heartbreaking stories each woman shared. Other couples were enduring
medical procedures, taking powerful hormones, borrowing money from
family to achieve pregnancies. Others were pursuing adoption, making
plans for international travel, or putting together albums to be viewed by
birth mothers. One by one the women stopped coming to the group as
they achieved pregnancy or were blessed with an adoption. New women

would come and go, yet I remained. I did not get encouragement from the group. Later I saw that my being there was part of God's plan to bring my husband and me to agreement regarding building our family. My prayer request was the same each month, "Please, God, change one of our hearts so we will be in agreement with Your will."

Slowly, my heart began to change. I started picturing a life without children. It was not a bad life, just different from what I had always pictured. Was God changing me? Was it *my* heart that needed to be changed? This was another step in giving God control.

One day Duane came to me and told me he was ready to pursue adoption. He had prayed and prayed about it and really felt God was telling him the time was right--we were supposed to proceed with adoption! I was elated. God had changed both of our hearts. He helped me find contentment where we were, and He gave my husband the courage to move forward. We had no idea where to begin.

After what seemed a long search, God led us to any agency who talked about God placing children in families and ministering to the hearts of the birth families. Other agencies talked about fees. As we attended the orientation of this agency, God changed my heart some more. I realized this was not all about us and our desire to become parents. It had everything to do with God's hand directing the lives of precious babies, birth moms, and families. They talked of a covenant between the birth mother and the adoptive couple. At that moment I no longer cared if we ever became parents. I was so moved by the work God was doing in this ministry. I thanked Him for the opportunity to see it in action. I knew without a doubt if God intended for us to be parents, He would make it happen through this agency. If that was not His plan for us, then His plans would be good, too. This was probably my biggest step in handing control over to God.

Almost six months later, we got the call to pray together about a baby. Our prayer had been that only the right birth mother would choose us, but it was hard to slow down and pray once one had actually chosen us. Before our prayers were hardly spoken, we received a message that our birth mother was in labor. Our daughter was born that Tuesday, just a little more than twenty-four hours after we knew of her existence.

However this birth mom had three "demands" about the couple who would raise her daughter. First, she wanted a notarized statement from our doctor that we could never conceive. Well, my husband has misshapen sperm that could not penetrate an egg. I have ovarian cysts and endometriosis. Guessed we passed that test.

She did not want the baby to know she was adopted. The caseworker very gently explained why, as an agency, they had made the policy not to keep the fact of adoption from the child. It was for her good. Almost any secret will eventually come to light, but if the child never remembers when she "first learned" she was adopted, it is a safe subject for discussion. It was then the birth mom shut off any more conversation with that caseworker.

The grandmother wanted to be able to send gifts to her only grandchild and to receive pictures during growing up years. She said to her daughter, "I know you don't want to be involved, but you are okay with me being connected. If I'm involved through the agency, with pictures and gifts, the child will wonder who I am."

The birth mom started to think, "Mom is right. She and I are connected. I can't stay out of it if mom is in it. That baby girl will know of her biological grandma. If she knows my mom through letters and gifts, and she knows she has been adopted, I can't stay invisible. Maybe it will be good not just for my daughter to know early on she was adopted; but she will also know that I had a LOT to do with who and where she is." "Okay, mom, I'll give up that request. But I still have one more."

The third demand was that we would use the name she had chosen for her daughter. This was important because it was the name of her dear grandmother. If we, as the adoptive couple, would not use that name, she would go to another couple. What she didn't know was we had already talked about names. We had made the decision to use the name the birth mom had given as a way of honoring her. We felt that would be a special gift she would receive from her birth mother. So, her first name is Mollie, the one given to her by her birth mom. We then chose a middle name, Grace. Our daughter would come to know, understand, and embrace the grace God has shown to all of us. Consequently, our attitude about the name was what sealed our relationship with the birth mother.

Originally she didn't want to meet us; but something stirred her to invite us –into the hospital room. The baby was lying on her mom's bed. That new mother looked at her baby girl and said, "This is your Mommy and Daddy. You are going home with them today."

God taught me another lesson. This one was compassion. She had said I was the baby's mommy!

She was so calm about it. That had to have taken more courage than I could imagine.

The birth mom was so touched we had chosen to use her grandmother's name for her daughter's first name. I think it really helped to open up a mutual relationship. Keeping the same name meant we would always share the same child, in a sense. Often, adoptive parents choose a different name without regard for the birth mom's choice. To us, it seemed strange for the birth mother to refer to her child by any name other than the one she had lovingly given the child at birth. We have never regretted that decision. We feel we can agree with those who compliment her on her name. We proudly say that is the name her birth mother gave her.

If I held that baby and then had to give her back…Whoa! My own emotions were saying, "If I was in the position of this birth mom, I could never place my baby in the arms of another woman." That thought is one I will never forget. God then sealed in me an irrevocable love and understanding for our birth mom. My heart grew in that moment as I experienced the size of her heart in spite of the pain that accompanied her decision.

We left the hospital with the plan to meet the caseworkers and our baby at the agency. Our emotions were as thin as tissue paper. What if the birth mother could not sign her relinquishment papers. We felt the baby belonged to us although the papers had not yet been signed. It was during this time that the old fears began to clutter our minds. The birth mom still had her God given "free will." We prayed for a miracle. We prayed for our birth mom's ability to do the right thing. Of course, "the right thing" in our minds was for her to sign the papers.

The wait was probably not more than thirty or forty minutes, but it seemed like an eternity. With this new-found love for a young woman whom we had met just a couple of hours before, we couldn't imagine she could sign the papers that would relinquish her rights as a mom, giving those rights to us.

Our caseworker returned with that beautiful baby girl. The signed papers were in her hand. This precious baby was going home with us that night. We spent time holding her, feeding her, kissing her, just drinking her in with amazement and gratitude. The caseworkers prayed with us and gave us time to really enjoy the moment. I remember when we left, one of the workers looked at our baby in her car seat and said, "Little girl, your whole destiny has completely changed forever." What powerful truths were in those words. The seriousness of our responsibility was settling in.

So, God gave me the desire of my heart, and He did make all things beautiful in His time. I knew, without a doubt, His time was best. I learned so much along our journey to this child that would make me a better person, wife, and mother. The sadness I had felt during our period of infertility was completely gone. I have never since felt like I missed out on anything by not being pregnant or giving birth. God hand-selected this beautiful child to be ours. He worked out the details in our lives as well as our birth mom's. What a beautiful story God put together to make us a family.

We were taught at the orientation to begin to pray for our birth mother and her baby. Of course, we didn't know her name then. But God did. Slightly before our daughter's first birthday we had a strong sense to pray for a future birth mother. After praying about three months we submitted our second family album to the same agency. By then our daughter was fifteen months old.

Again, we prayed that only the right birth mother, chosen by God, would be interested in our album. The call about another baby girl came just three months later. I was shocked! I hadn't even started to wonder when we might get a call. We felt God say, "Move forward." It was much sooner than we had expected, but the idea of two little girls so close in age was very exciting. This new birth mom always thought having a sister close to her age would have been a special treat.

When talking with our caseworker, we learned the birth mother planned to give her a name Olivia which means "peace" and "one who walks with God." How perfect. We responded, "Tell her we will definitely use that name." We will keep our tradition of honoring our birth mothers' first gift to her baby.

This birth mother had seriously considered parenting. Her parents said they would support her decision either way, but they would not parent the child for her. She loved her baby so much. She knew in her heart she wanted her baby to have a mommy and a daddy, but the idea of saying goodbye brought excruciating pain.

Our caseworker talked to us just as she had the first time, encouraging us to pray about receiving this child. Then our caseworker said, "Guard your hearts. This is not over until it is over. She may decide to parent."

I said, "You told us that the last time, but I didn't like that idea. If I guard my heart, I can't enjoy the anticipation. Guarded or not, I was still going to be devastated if this adoption did not happen for us. I would tell all our friends and family about the possibility and ask them to pray with us. If it fell through, they would grieve and cry with us. We would all hurt, but we would get over it."

She said she liked our idea better. She now uses it with every prospective adoption… a guarded heart can miss the joy.

Our second daughter was born on April 6, 2005, shortly after our first daughter turned seventeen months old. When she was four days old, we were called and told the placement meeting had been scheduled for that afternoon. Words cannot describe our relief and excitement.

We were told a story from earlier that morning. As this birth mom's dad was preparing their car to go to the placement of his granddaughter, he had noticed a woman and her two daughters "They don't have a daddy, and those girls are doing just fine!" he had thought to himself. Just then the younger of the two children turned and smiled at him. She was wearing a shirt that said, "Daddy's Little Girl." He told his family God was trying to reassure him with the message on that shirt; they were doing the right thing. A mommy and a daddy was God's original plan for children.

As we signed our papers, we were told our birth mom had already signed hers. She had shared with our caseworker, as she signed, it was not really all that hard. She had already signed the papers in her heart a few days before. Wow! That taught us a great deal about this young woman's bravery and maturity.

At the placement the biological parents prepared an eloquent ceremony with thoughtful words and prayers. It was all so meaningful, as well as difficult. This young mom cradled her baby in her arms. The love for that child was electric in that room.

Some how we all knew when it was time to say good-bye. Our baby was placed in her new daddy's arms. Her birth mom hugged him, and thanked him for being her daddy. She hugged me and thanked me for loving her child. As we drove away from that scene, our hearts were heavy for this family whose hearts must have felt ripped out as they let go of this precious child. Personally, I felt like we had torn this child out of that young girl's heart and arms.

Two very different adoptions, both orchestrated by God and planned perfectly by Him. "We have two babies!" I frequently said in awestruck amazement! We had expected to wait at least two years for our first baby and probably that much time between babies. Two years and two weeks after our introduction to this agency, we brought home our second baby girl. So many amazed people have asked me how we managed to do that. I take none of the credit. It was God who worked out all the details.

I now look at our beautiful girls and cannot imagine their lives without one another. The love between them is precious. Together, they are best friends. We are still amazed by the changes in our own lives, and we are so grateful to our dear birth mothers. Our girls are still too young to comprehend who these special women are and the beautiful gift of life given to them. Yet, from the moment we started rocking them in our arms, we have talked with them about their birth mothers. We always want them to know that adoption is a positive part of their lives. It is not some big secret they discover later in life. Adoption does not define who they are, but it is a special part of their roots. How blessed they are to be loved by our family but also loved by both of their birth families.

We actually consider both birth families as our extended family. We exchange letters and pictures through the agency, even though we don't know one another's last names or addresses. The girls will not meet their birth families until they make that decision themselves as adults. On the other hand, we adults have the privilege of meeting with our birth families every November at the agency's annual banquet. Adoptive families sit with birth moms, their parents, and sometimes extended family at a big round table for the "family reunion." We love our extended family.

Although our family was not fashioned the way I had planned it, God's plans were far more spectacular than anything I could have ever dreamed. He did give me the desires of my heart and made us into the most beautiful family…in His time. I know in my heart these little girls are not truly ours. They belong to God. Yet, He has blessed us with the privilege of raising them. He is the One in control.

PETER AND PATRICIA

When I spoke with Patricia one day, I asked her about showing her family's "life-book" to one of our pregnant girls. As we talked, she asked about other pregnant girls she might pray for. When I mentioned "Nancy," Patricia got very quiet. Later she said she knew an unusual connection had just happened in her spirit concerning Nancy.

When I had a meeting with Nancy to show her several books from prospective adoptive couples, we went over each one without hurrying, never skipping any detail of any book. Nancy chose two life-books that day. Her first choice was "Jim and Charlene." Her second choice was "Peter and Patricia." I had other engagements which kept me from calling Nancy's first choice that day, and before I got a chance, Nancy had called to tell me she was mistaken. Her "real and right couple" was Peter and Patricia.

So, Patricia had gotten the message "spiritually" before Nancy had, and over the next five years, we all saw that God had indeed chosen the "perfect" couple for this child.

A PRAYER OF THANKSGIVING FOR ZOE

Dearest Heavenly Father,

You have entrusted this precious baby to our family's care, just as You entrusted her mother to us so many years ago. Thank you for this mind that we might help mold it, this body to help nurture it, and this spirit to help enrich it. We promise to love, protect, and comfort her. Let Your grace and love fall on Zoe. Give her inner strength, peace, and patience for the journey ahead. We know You answer prayers, Lord. Thank You for answering ours.

Zoe Brook

It seems to me that it would be impossible to tell how our lives have changed in the last two weeks. There are the obvious things like spit-up on my shirts, typing with a baby on one arm, bottles and nipples all over the house, baby socks and bows scattered on table tops, and piles and piles of gifts from family and friends. I have never seen so much pink! It is my new favorite color!

What I could not have anticipated is how much she has changed my life. My priorities are all different from what they were just a few weeks ago! I love to kiss her soft feet, hands, cheeks, belly, head, and lips. I adore the little noises she makes when she is drinking and how her little hand wraps around my fingers when I feed her. I love when she looks up at me with those big brown eyes. I am thrilled when the sound of my voice can calm her. I think it is great when she burps. I love making up songs about how Jesus and everyone loves her while we rock in her room at 2:00 a.m. I love that it feels so natural to say she is "home." I love that my parents are over here every single day, several times a day. I love going to the photo store every three days to develop new pictures, totaling 300 already within these last two weeks. I am happy to eat cereal and bread at home, instead of fancy work lunches. I love how her lips pout slightly when she sleeps. It is fabulous to watch her slowly drift off to sleep in my arms as she looks up at me. Her tongue is so cute when she sticks it out when she is tired or sleepy. I love it when she smiles at me, even though (at this age) it is probably only gas!

No one could have prepared me for how much I would love this little baby angel princess. I am totally in love with her. Never doubt how long we waited and prayed for her or how deeply she is loved now that she is in my arms.

I am deeply blessed. God has exceeded my expectations of what motherhood would be. It is hard to remember my life before her and impossible to think of it without her.

The single most important lesson I have learned from Zoe Brooke is "sacrificial love." I always knew I would love a child, but I did not know the depths of emotions I would feel until I finally met this one.

Anyone can say, "I love you," but it is the actions behind those words that have made me a far different person than I was five months ago. Of course I love Zoe Brooke, but I am amazed to find myself putting her first without even thinking. When she is not sleeping through the night and I am tired, and most likely I won't be able to go back to sleep for a few hours, I still get up to comfort her back to sleep. Sometimes it takes a few seconds, to give her a passie, and sometimes it takes a few minutes to burp her, and sometimes it takes hours for no apparent reason, holding her is all that helps. The reality is, I am deeply rewarded in the small hours of the morning, when no one else it up. It is just she and I together. I hold her close to my face. I bring her tightly to my chest and hum softly onto her cheek to feel her relax in my arms. I see her smile up at me, and then I watch her drift back to sleep. It is more rewarding to me than a few hours of sleep.

I used to shop for myself. Now it is way more fun to shop for ZB. I have had so much fun dressing her up.

When she watches me walk out the door and waits for me to come back, when she grins up at me when she wakes up, when she imitates my facial expressions, when she tries to talk to me, all of these little things are so much more rewarding than I ever could have imagined. She is loved and cared for more than any of us could have imagined and more than I knew I was capable of.

God knows we were meant to raise Zoe Brooke and that this was better for us than carrying a child ourselves. I do not know what He has planned for all of us from here, but I am sure it is wonderful! I cannot pray for Zoe without thinking of her birth mom in the same minute. Everything I hope for ZB, I pray for that young woman as well. I love her. Thank you, Lord!

A year and a half later, I ran across a book by Marianne Richmond that made me cry. This poem from the book articulates so well how I feel about Zoe Brooke.

I love you as brilliant as each sparkling star,
And as way out as space, I love you that far.
I love you as gigantic as a great lion's roar,
And as deep as the ocean, I love you that more.
"That is a lot," you say, "but how did it start?
WHERE did love come from to be in your heart?"
YOU put it there, really, when you and I met.
And I knew for certain without you I'd fret.
From my head to my toes, I was feeling inside
A devotion for you so deep and so wide
And now it's enormous and wonderfully real
And hard to describe how much I feel!
You're my sweetie, my dear, my smile and laughter.
You're my playmate for always and my joy ever after.
I love you near or far.
I love you high or low.
My love is with you wherever you may go."

I desperately want to remember how wonderful I feel when she automatically reaches up and wraps her little hand around my finger:

When we walk in the grass in the yard
When we walk across the street to the field
When she leads me to the pantry to feed the dog
When she leads me to my bedroom when I say we are going to do our nails
When we walk down a dark hall
When we walk through the gym to the kid's room
When we go up/down stairs/curbs as we both verbally say "up" and "down"

She is already growing too fast. There is so much I don't want to forget about each age. Because each is so precious.

ABIGAIL

"Delight yourself in the Lord and He will give you the desires of your heart." Psalm 37:4

"Now to Him who is able to do immeasurably more than all we ask or imagine, according to His power that is at work in us, to Him be glory in the church and in Christ Jesus throughout all generations, for ever and ever." Eph 3:20.

During their courting days in college Jim and Christi's open communication created an intimacy that drew them together uniquely. Adoption was a topic in which they agreed. They talked of what it would be like to have a multiracial family through adoption. Their plans were to have a few of their own first, then adopt several babies of a variety of "flavors." God slowly, and gently, cultivated this desire to adopt over a period of more than ten years. Truly, the mind of man plans his ways but the Lord directs his steps.

They married before he had finished graduate school. The birth control pills made Christi sick, so they prayed that God would hold off pregnancy until graduation and they were more settled with paid employment.

After graduation, Jim began working for Texas Instruments. They thought they were ready. Nothing happened. The convenient relief of not being pregnant soon turned into a cycle of anxiety and disappointment. As they got involved and comfortable within a church body, new friends began to pray for their fertility situation. Jim and Christi thought it was time for tests to isolate the physiological problem. It turned out that Jim was "shooting blanks," as they say here in Texas.

It didn't take long before any discussion of fertility became very painful for Jim. He said he did the only thing any self-respecting American male with a low sperm count would do, stuff the pain and act like it didn't matter.

He had found the simple diagnostics of the fertility testing demeaning enough to repulse him from the idea of seeking a test-tube solution. He met a coworker who had done the Invitro Fertilization procedure. As they spoke about it, Jim said he felt his spirit grieve within him. At the mention of "icing the extra embryos," he actually became physically sick. All this coincided with a period in which Christi seemed to bring up the fertility issue, in one form or another, on a daily basis. One evening Jim lost his cool and snapped, "I can't get you pregnant; I can't afford to buy you a baby; I don't ever want to have kids; and I don't want to discuss it again!"

Jim admitted it was his wounded ego that had caused him to be so cruel to his wife whom he loved. It also caused him to have added guilt for the way he had hurt her. He knew his commitment to Promise Keepers was where he would get a "word" from God through the other guys. These men encouraged him to pray and to **do something**. The first step was to ask Christi to forgive his outburst. He loved her dearly. Yet, he had broken her heart with his words. The surprise, even to him, was that as he was asking for forgiveness, the words out of Jim's mouth were, "I am about to get serious about adoption."

From there it seemed everywhere Jim and Christi went, everyone they met had information for them as well as experiences of their own about adoption. Even television shows seemed to address adoption in one way or another. What they were learning from the experiences of friends, told an entirely different story from what they were seeing on the tube. Only bad new is news for the media. Jim and Christi were learning that what was on TV was an exaggeration of an extremely small number of adoptions. Television does not show what God is doing.

Jim and Christi did not hesitate to begin asking questions of everyone. Looking back, they realized their utter ignorance, specifically about adoption and generally about parenthood. They were sponges absorbing all they heard. Their efforts led them to Loving Alternative Adoption Agency, a small Christian agency a few hours from their home. This was not just an agency. It was a ministry to any young woman who found herself in an "unplanned pregnancy." The staff got no salaries. They were missionaries supported by friends and/or churches.

This is where the suggestion to "do something" got them going. The journey began. Complete the scrapbook. The young mothers look over these picture albums in an effort to choose the family that is just right for her child. Looking at couples through their scrapbooks and reading their autobiographies is one of the more exciting events for a young woman once she feels adoption is the path she will walk. They had things to do to get ready for what they now felt was the way God would build their family. Besides the above, they needed to get a home study, attend the orientation, and save for the adoption fee. Their "to do" list seemed to be quite long, but "doing something" was good. After all that was completed, the next job was to wait. That was the hardest part. As they waited, they prayed, and waited some more. During this time, they would later learn God was busy creating miracles in fast succession showing them His best work.

Jim said that it was during the orientation that their eyes were opened. God used the testimonies of birth mothers, adoptive parents, and agency staff to show God's power in adoption. One testimony in particular had a profound impact on several of the men who were in attendance. As a birth mother, who had placed her daughter for adoption, told her story, couples had their hearts opened to the grief and pain that enveloped birth moms in order for *them* to become parents though adoption. It didn't seem a fair exchange.

In reality, the Christ-like sacrifice that a birth mother must make to place her baby in the arms of another, is done not out of rejection, but of sacrificial love. Both Jim and Christi knew that their birth mother would be honored in their home. The child would be the constant reminder of that commitment.

Most couples proliferate their search for a baby by being involved with several agencies. These couples feel multiple agencies would give them more exposure and quicken their chances for a match with a birth family. Anything was worth a try to speed the process for the desired child. Jim and Christi felt God's hand so strongly in what Loving Alternative was doing, they decided they would stick with that agency however long it took.

Jim and Christi's relationship actually grew and they became closer than they had ever been as they journeyed the path to adoption.

Isaiah 54 from the Bible,(in part) spoke personally to Christi, "Sing, O barren woman, you who never bore a child; burst into song, shout for joy, you who were never in labor; because more are the children of the desolate woman than of her who has a husband," says the Lord. "Enlarge the place of your tent, stretch your tent curtains wide, do not hold back; lengthen your cords, strengthen your stakes. For you will spread out to the right and to the left."

Finally they were selected by a birth mother to parent her child.

In Texas, birth fathers must relinquish their parental rights the same as the birth mother does. In this case, the birth dad was very reserved as the adoption counselor asked him about his background. He told her his mother had died when he was thirteen. The next bit of information to come forward was his relationship with his own father. This relationship had deteriorated and so had his relationship with God. As he became comfortable with the caseworker, he opened up even more. His desire was for his daughter to have Christian parents. In light of that, he decided to sign away his paternal rights. It can often be difficult to get the birth father to meet with the agency staff, much less to get him to waive his rights. This birth father's cooperation was another miracle.

The birth mother and the birth father's relationship was short-lived. They did not get along, but they did agree on one thing. From the beginning, abortion was not an option.

The birth mother willingly signed over her maternal rights. When Jim and Christi met her, they saw her heart for her daughter. She expressed the hope she was investing in this couple.

At last they got to meet their new daughter, Abigail Joy. In Hebrew, Abigail means "A Father's Joy." Jim's wounded ego, the embarrassment of his infertility, the demeaning tests, and his cruel behavior to his wife, all disappeared in "a father's joy" as Jim held Abigail in his arms. The journey to adoption was coming to an end. A new journey was beginning. Becoming parents had been a desire delayed, but now it was a true JOY fulfilled. They had successfully walked through the long circuit to adoption once. Jim and Christi knew that with God's help Abigail would one day have a sibling through that same miracle.

MIRIAM'S STORY

"For everyone born of God overcomes the world. This is the victory that has overcome the world, even our faith." I JOHN 5:4

Miriam Faith was born on November 17, 2000. She came home on December 1, 2000.

We had an emotional roller-coaster-ride surrounding Miriam's birth and homecoming, but through it all, God remained faithful. We found out about Miriam in early October. I was at a women's retreat when my husband got the call. The birth mom had picked us when she was 'kicked" by the baby in her tummy while holding our photo album. Maybe it was really Miriam who had picked us.

Like our first, this adoption had its highs and its lows. We felt we were on a roller coaster. Part of the story was like a lot of others. We were chosen. The birth parents had made the decision to place their baby for adoption, then they changed their minds, and finally another change of mind. We called out the forces to pray. People we didn't even know were praying for us and for Miriam. It was a hard time of waiting, but we knew Miriam was to become a part of our family. Eventually, their decision settled with adoption, and our second baby girl came to be a part of our family.

During the times when it looked as if Miriam would not join our family, we prayed for Miriam's safety and that God would put someone in her life to teach her about Himself.

Through all of this, God had reminded us of His faithfulness. He had shown us a glimpse of the pain He went through when God the Father and Jesus were separated by the sins of us all on the cross. We could endure a similar pain, for the joy set before us. We saw this through witnessing the love and pain Miriam's birth parents experienced in making their decision. Miriam was in our arms. Abbi, her sister, was the first to hold her. They are as different as salt and pepper, but they are best friends.

God has truly given us a legacy to pass on to Miriam. Her name means "longed for." She will know we longed for her, and that her birth parents longed to give her the best upbringing they could through an adoption plan.

Miriam's middle name is Faith. Miriam will see through our lives that even when circumstances look impossible, God is faithful and we must cling to Him. Miracles are ever available through our Father God.

BLAKE'S ADOPTION STORY

"Give thanks to the LORD, call on his name; make known among the nations what he has done." I Chronicles 16:8

The most amazing, miraculous part of our story is that our first baby was placed into our arms on November 14th, the anniversary of the day my husband was adopted into God's family. God's timing is always perfect...but I am getting ahead of myself.

Our adoption story is full of God's grace, mercy, and faithfulness. Our birth family loved our son so much, they made the hardest, and most unselfish, decision possible--adoption. They wanted him to be in a loving Christian home with a mother and a father.

Our journey to adoption began much like many other couples. We were married for three years and then tried to conceive for another five years. We had exhausted all our human efforts when we finally turned the situation over to God. We knew our God had a plan for us, and we needed to follow His direction and leading.

A friend of mine who knew our situation and our desire for a baby, told us about a small Christian adoption agency. We were excited to attend their orientation and learn all about the adoption process. It seemed like a great idea, but very few babies (eight) were placed for adoption the previous year. We weren't very encouraged

In cases like ours, when the word gets around, possibilities seem to come from everywhere. Through a series of events, we learned of a sixteen-year-old girl who was pregnant and considering adoption. This girl happened to be living at the maternity home which was part of the same agency that conducted the adoption orientation. This was too "coincidental" for God not to be working in it.

We had attended the orientation but had not followed through with putting together our scrapbook. Then we got a call from the adoption worker saying they had a girl who had looked through all the couples they had and hadn't found her couple. Could we get ours together for her? This was encouraging. We worked quickly on our family profile and wrote a letter to the birth mother. We waited patiently. Two weeks later the phone call came. We were picked, and we were finally going to be parents…to a baby boy. We were thrilled!

On November 11, 1999, we were scheduled to meet our birth mom and her mother for the first time. Her mother was coming into town to go with her daughter to the doctor. She was seven weeks from her due date. We were all surprised to find out she was already in labor and was immediately admitted to the hospital. Everything was moving so fast.

While our birth mom was in labor, we were asked to meet and visit with her mom. She really wanted to meet us before the baby was born. It was a wonderful time of sharing our hearts and even sharing the name we had chosen for the baby. We would give him a name that had been our favorite for some years. It seemed to go well with our last name. One book of baby names said this name means a "harmonizer who is blessed of God." We wanted to give him names that would represent the strong Christian heritage from which he came.

Later that evening we received a phone call that the baby had been born and that he was healthy and beautiful. He had big hands and feet. We could not wait to see him. We knew it would probably be three days before we could meet him because of the time required by law before parental rights could be waived. This was our birth mom's time to spend with her baby before the adoption took place. We prayed for her during this special but difficult time. Surprisingly, the next day we were invited to the hospital to finally meet her for the first time. What a brave, mature, young girl she was. We admired and loved her so much for the precious gift she was giving us. We both felt a close connection with her that only God could have given. We will always cherish and appreciate that time with her.

As we were visiting in her hospital room, her sister asked if we wanted to see the baby. We were not expecting this. We walked down the hallway. There he was, all bundled up and oh so beautiful. Her sister put him in my arms. He was so perfect. The baby for which we had prayed was finally in my arms. I was so full of joy, and my love for him was instant. What a precious gift from God.

We prayed so hard for this brave birth mom during these first three days after delivery. We surprised ourselves with the unselfish prayers that came out of our mouths. God had given us such a love for her that the prayers were all for her well-being. We wanted God to fill her with His grace and mercy. We also prayed for God's will for the baby. I could not even imagine being in her shoes and how difficult this would be. She had become such a strong, mature Christian during her pregnancy; we trusted she would follow God's leading, even if it meant she would not place her baby with us.

Sunday afternoon was considered "placement" day. The baby would be handed over from his birth mom to us. We knew this would be very emotional for everyone. At this point we were truly grieving for her and feeling her deep hurt and loss. I think we were relieved when they called and said her aunt would be handing the baby over to us instead of his biological mom. The birth mom just couldn't handle actually handing him over to us.

We met that Sunday afternoon at the adoption agency. Our birth mom's aunt was holding the baby when we arrived. We visited a while, and then she finally handed the baby to me. He was really ours. It felt so good to hold our little son. I fed him and the adoption workers took tons of pictures. It was such an incredible experience of God's faithfulness and love for us.

We then said our good byes and took our son home. Many of our friends and family were there waiting to help us celebrate. They had a "Welcome Home Baby" cake for us. This was one of the most joyful days of our lives and we will never forget it.

Three wonderful years went by before we felt we were ready for another baby. We were celebrating our twelfth wedding anniversary on a cruise to Bermuda when I realized my monthly menses had not started. Something felt different. I waited until we returned home and privately took a pregnancy test. I could not believe my eyes. I really was pregnant!

Three and a half years after the adoption of our first son, his baby brother was born. We were so blessed. We were given the honor and joy of experiencing the miracle of adoption before God opened my womb to experience the pregnancy and birth of our second son. Upon hearing this, folks sometimes say, "That always happens." I must inform them it does *not* always happen. Statistics show that only twenty percent of families will conceive after adoption. So, again, it was God performing yet another miracle in our family. What an awesome God we have!

GOD MAKES A WAY

"For my thoughts are not your thoughts, neither are your ways my ways," declares the LORD.

"As the heavens are higher than the earth, so are my thoughts than your thoughts." Isaiah 55:8-9.

"If you believe, you will receive whatever you ask for in prayer." Mathew 21:22

Our story is a lot like many others. We had *our* plans, *our* timing, *our* disappointments, *our* learning from *our* experiences, and then *our* waiting for the miracle from God. The question we asked ourselves was "Does God really perform miracles today?"

When my husband and I got married, we knew there was a slight chance we would be unable to have a child. My husband had suffered from Wilm's Tumor (cancer) when he was three years old. His cancer doctors told us there would probably be no problem, but we should be prepared for disappointment just in case we couldn't conceive. We talked about it and decided if there was a problem, we would look into adopting a child. But our desire to give birth to our own biological child became so intense, we began to deny the possibility we might be unable to conceive. I think both of us were convinced we would have no problems.

Early on we were the typical American couple. We would get our lives, careers, home, and "stuff" together before we would start our family. Wasn't it smart to really get to know each other as husband and wife before we added children into the mix? Children were not a topic of conversation for the first couple of years.

I seemed to have a problem remembering to take my birth control pills. My husband asked why we were paying for them, if I couldn't remember to take them. So, I quit taking them altogether. I fully expected to be pregnant within a month or two. As the months and years went by without prevention and still no pregnancy, we thought the Lord might be trying to tell us something. Perhaps that doctor, all those years ago, was right. The cancer had sterilized my husband. The specialist suggested we try in-vitro fertilization or donor sperm. Neither of us felt comfortable with either of those decisions. Additionally, we didn't feel the Lord leading us to do anything else medically.

One Sunday in church, we decided to share the information with our Sunday school class. After class, one of our friends asked if we had ever thought about adoption. She had a friend who had adopted two children from a Christian agency. She said she would contact her friend about us if we agreed. We said, "Sure." Later that afternoon, she called to let us know her friend had given our names to their caseworker from the agency. If we were interested, we needed to call immediately. Their once-a-year prospective adoptive couples orientation was scheduled for the following weekend. Attendance was a requirement for qualification to adopt. It was also an opportunity to learn more about adoption in general and about that agency specifically.

We had no idea what to expect at the orientation, but we knew God had led us there! When we walked in, we felt completely welcome. It was such an extraordinary experience. We realized what amazing work God was doing through this agency! We were able to gain a better understanding of adoption through the Bible, as well as through testimonies from birth mothers and adoptive couples who shared. We left there knowing the Lord had a plan for us. We were so thankful to finally feel like we could move forward with our dream of becoming parents.

We met the eligibility requirements, had done the first two sets of paper work, had attended the orientation, and knew this was the agency God had brought into our lives. The agency would send for our references, get the FBI clearance, and schedule our home study. We needed to be available for the four appointments for the home study, put together a scrapbook of our lives, and write our autobiographies.

It was good to be busy. When all of that was completed, next came the hardest part…waiting. We had asked the agency workers how long the average wait was. They said, "There is no average." They said they were not in charge of who gets what baby. The birth parents choose their couple from the scrapbook. God always shows them the perfect couple. So, we attempted to go on with life. We continued to pray that the Lord would take care of us, and we knew everything was in His hands.

Part of going on with life was taking a construction mission trip with our church in early August. A few days after our return, one of the agency workers called to let us know we had been chosen by a couple and their son had been born the previous Sunday. Our next task was to pray. We needed to hear from God a confirmation that agreed with the birth couple. Were we really the parents for this child? Miracle of miracles, we felt the impression from God to move ahead.

Our son had come five weeks early, so he surprised everyone. He had not learned to swallow yet, so he would remain in the hospital until that situation was fixed. The time extended to nearly ten days. (The agency workers recalled another premature baby who had a swallowing deficiency that lasted for several months.) They said that they, very informally, prayed God would teach this child to swallow more quickly. Miraculously, within a few hours, a call came from the hospital saying they were releasing Andrew. He was now taking the requisite amount of formula via bottle. Those initial ten days gave the birth parents the chance to visit him every day, helping him learn to swallow, and generally bonding with him before they placed him with us. We learned how important it can be for the birth family to bond with love initially if they expected a healthy post-placement grieving time.

When we met our precious birth parents, we fell in love with them. The longer we talked with them, the more we knew the Lord had brought us together. It seemed such a "God thing." We learned we had so much in common. It became evident that this little boy was the child God had made just for us. Upon discussing names, we told our birth parents that we loved the names they had chosen, and we thought we would call him by the initials of his first and middle name. They laughed because our birth father had been calling him that just the previous night in the hospital. We had a great time visiting with each other at the time of placement and could once again feel the Lord's presence. We knew this was His plan from the start.

We brought Andrew home to many family and friends anxious to see him. We had many visitors over the next few days coming to bring us more gifts and to meet the newest member of our family.

Soon after placement, our caseworker shared with us that our birth mother had asked the Lord Jesus to come into her life. We had been fervently praying for our birth parents since we had met them and this was an answer to our prayers.

Not only is our son our miracle from the Lord, but our birth parents are as well. We have been so blessed with what the Lord has done, and we love to share with anyone who will listen how precious our son and our birth parents are. We have been able to tell many people about our experience of adoption and how the Lord worked through the whole process. Often people ask how hard it must be to have contact with our birth parents and their families. We don't understand that concept. For us, it is a blessing! Our son can never have too many people who love him and want to see how the Lord will use him. What a blessing it will be for Andrew to know how much he is loved. The pictures and letters that are exchanged between all of us over the years are tangible proof of that love. Why would we ever want it any other way? Andrew is now three years old, and these past years have been the most joyful and wonderful experiences of our lives. We look at him and are still amazed at what the Lord has done.

"If you believe, you will receive whatever you ask for in prayer." Matthew 21:22.

WES AND SUE

Birth parents, Jack and Jill, were involved in this pregnancy and adoption together. Jill had the stronger personality, but Jack was comfortable with what Jill wanted. Jill was looking for a strong charismatic Christian family who gave priority to prayer. Her reasoning was, the "generational choices" in her family background she didn't want passed on to her daughter. She believed a strong praying couple would take all concerns to the Lord and assure her daughter would live in freedom from any possible bondage from her biological family.

Jill's family was very musical; her parents had met in college when they were both majoring in music. Her dad still wrote music, and her mother taught several musical instruments to young people. Jill, herself, could play seven instruments by the time she was in middle school.

Adoptive parents, Wes and Sue, had a strong burden for prayer. Sue's mother had died early, and Sue had never heard her own mother pray. So, they were determined their child would know that "in this family, prayer was a way of life."

They learned of Jill's musical background, and although they were not musical themselves, from the beginning of their adopted daughter' life, they played music throughout the day. If a CD was not playing, a Veggie Tale music video was on the tube.

When Wes and Sue sat down to dinner, they usually talked "a mile a minute" trying to bring each other up-to-date on each of their day's experiences. One evening, when "Ruthie" was about nine months old, she was sitting in her high chair at the table. All of a sudden, Wes and Sue stopped their talking because they realized Ruthie was humming a tune from one of the Veggie Tales videos. Wes and Sue recognized the tune!

Wasn't it wonderful that Wes and Sue had background information they could use to build into Ruthie's life, based on a gift that was put into Ruthie from her biological family? It is similar to Moses' story. God used the biological background (Hebrew) of Moses, along with the adoptive Egyptian influence of his formative years, to make Moses into the man with God's call on his life. With both, he was the man God used to set His people free and to take them into the Promised Land.

THEN THERE WERE TEN

"Children are a gift from God; Children born to a young man are like sharp arrows to defend him. Happy is the man who has his quiver full of them." Psalm 127:3-5

"You must teach God's commandments to your children and talk about them when you are at home or out for a walk; at bedtime and the first thing in the morning." Deuteronomy 6:7

Some couples are childless. Others have nine. Who decides how many children will be in each family? Maybe it depends on the size of the family's quiver. No, this is not an episode of the Brady Bunch; it is the true story of an adoptive family.

After lunch fifteen-year-old, Isaac, is cleaning up the table, putting the leftovers away, and dishing out dessert. Meanwhile, Lindsay and Kara have taken their guest out to the barn to visit the puppies and kittens. These early-teen girls are raising animals to sell. Their goal is to save enough money to purchase a pony for each of them.

Matthew, Elizabeth, and Katie have finished high school and are out on their own. Lindsey, Isaac, and Sarah are exploring mission trip possibilities versus college scholarships. Five-year-old Tillie, and nine-year-old Seth, are busy with their schoolwork. It is evident that Monte and Toni have raised up these children "in the way they should go." Hands-on home schooling and networking with a home schoolers' support group has, without a doubt, developed admirable characteristics in these children.

Are you imagining the whirlwind of activity in this home? Where does an adoption miracle enter? It all started when they heard a message at their church. The talk centered on abortion, unwanted children, and orphans. Monte and Toni remembered the old movie, "Cheaper by The Dozen." Their hearts were stirred with compassion, and they knew God was directing them to find that one child He had (or was preparing) for them to adopt. They lovingly thought, "Let's make it an even ten."

Sarah had gone on a missions trip to China. As she visited an orphanage, she fell in love with a young girl, Haley. On her return, as she shared pictures and Haley's story with her parents, the whole family just knew they should pursue the adoption of this beautiful girl.

Monte and Toni soon learned China had a one-child per family rule. When that country learned Monte and Toni had nine children, it was unthinkable they would consider letting go of one of their orphans to a family of that size.

Thus began the long, and often discouraging, journey for Monte and Toni to find that special, perfectly fitted child for their family.

The Philippines was ruled out for reasons similar to China's. Additionally, the Philippine government wanted to place children with families in their own nation.

The next attempt was in Guatemala. Each attempt meant more paper work, home study up-dates, and INS deadlines. Guatemala seemed to be the best possibility. Two months into that process, Guatemala fell into major political conflict over the Hague Treaty. This was an international treaty concerning adoption. It caused the adoption process in Guatemala to completely shut down. After four months, the restrictions were lifted. When they caught up after the huge backlog, Monte and Toni continued their pursuit of Daniela Desiree from Guatemala.

Finally, on January 28, 2004, Daniela Desiree, soon to be renamed, AnaVictoria Desiree, joined this family. She was eleven months old and became their tenth child. Her adoption was finalized in Guatemala, and they were given permission to travel to get her on February 14, a most wonderful Valentine's Day.

After only one month in their home, it was apparent how God's hand had been on the whole process to lead them to the child He had planned for their family. AnaVictoria had so easily and perfectly fit into her new family. She had a way of drawing every sibling to herself with her sweet, pleasant, easy-going temperament.

Now, six years later, she is still quite a girl. The family admits they have spoiled her "a little." One can hardly help it when she is the baby of a family with so many older siblings. Still, she is a sweet girl who is eager to please and loves her family very much.

Monte and Toni see God's handiwork in their miracle of AnaVictoria. And, indeed, their quiver is full!

HOPE FULFILLED

"And not only this, but we rejoice in our trials, because trials bring perseverance; and perseverance, proven character; and proven character, hope; and hope does not disappoint us because God has poured His love into our hearts, through His Holy Spirit whom He has given us." Romans 5:3-5

Because of our compassion for this child who would be coming into our family, we wanted to do anything and everything we could to help her through the transition. She would find nothing familiar in these new surroundings. The culture, the food, the scents, the living conditions, the language, and even the alphabet would all be far removed from what life had been in Kazakhstan. We thought that the one thing we could do to help the most was to learn some Russian, her native language. Miraculously, we were able to pick up enough of the language, without an American accent, to communicate with our new daughter during our first hours, days, weeks, and even months.

Getting to this point was a long journey filled with adventure, along with some disappointments. In 1994, through a series of events, we found the Lord was calling us to an international adoption. We sensed His leading, but we could not see how He would complete it, as our house was full with three biological children. We did not have the money to move, add-on, or adopt. In 2001, we found ourselves moving 1,000 miles from our home in Minnesota down to Texas. The first Sunday at our new church, a woman spoke saying she was trying to place some orphans from half-way around the world. We wondered if God had been preparing us for this time. We obeyed and moved ahead with adoption arrangements and paperwork.

God provided every step of the way. He provided new employment when Mike lost his original job. He provided amazing opportunities to talk with people who had met our new daughter in her country. By His leading, we named her Hope. Later, we found out miraculously that was the English name the orphanage had given her the year before. We completed our paperwork and sent it in only to find she had been adopted by another family, just weeks before.

We were heartbroken. We asked God why and wondered if He was still calling us to adopt. We felt He wanted us to proceed. I called a different agency whose "waiting child" list I had been watching. There was a six-year-old girl who had been on the list for five months waiting for a family. I asked about her only to find out her name was Alma, and another family had just chosen her.

We again waited for God's leading. At this point, we felt we were out of options. Two weeks later, the coordinator for the above agency called us back and asked if we wanted to look at Alma's file. The previous family had backed out. We proceeded to look at her medical reports and file. She was born a month early, in a remote area of Kazakhstan, with no neo-natal care facilities. They worried she would most definitely have learning disabilities and health issues. They said she had a heart murmur and had never been to the dentist. We felt she was meant to be our child, so we told the agency we would take her. Our Scripture verse (Romans 5:3-5) became more real to us as we asked God to equip us to be her parents. Our whole family, with three biological children, watched her video over and over until it was nearly worn out.

In February of 2003, we traveled to Kazakhstan and returned after three weeks with our new daughter, Zoe (Alma) which means "life." She was six, but her size was that of a four year old. Her first year in our home was full of miracles as we watched her grow. She grew seven inches in twelve months! We took her to the dentist, and she had NO CAVITIES. Her "heart murmur" turned out to be nothing. She learned how to read and was enthralled with animals and animal facts.

Although in Kazakhstan she had little or no contact with spiritual things, she seemed to be sensitive to them from the beginning. On one occasion as she learned how to be kind to someone who was not kind to her, we told her we were proud of her. She asked if we thought God was proud of her. We assured her He was. She accepted the Lord as her personal Savior shortly before the first anniversary of her adoption day.

Two years after adopting Zoe, we were thinking of adopting again. She was quite lonely at times, as her closest sibling was a five-year-old boy.

We initially wanted to return to Kazakhstan, but the program there had become very long and very expensive. We decided to give China another try. We asked to be on their special needs list. Many times they would receive older children who were healthy but had special needs because of their age.

Two years passed. We still prayed asking God what He would have us do. I wanted to adopt again. Mike wanted to pursue full-time missions. We prayed, believing it was God's desire for us to be in agreement. In the spring of 2007, God confirmed with Mike saying, "Let's look into adoption one more time." I checked the waiting lists of my favorite agencies. There was a seven-year-old Chinese girl on one list. The agency sent her medical records that Monday. We prayed, wondering how God would complete this adoption with no money. By Thursday, we had committed to being her parents, believing God would complete what He had asked us to do. We sent out letters to friends and family asking for help with our adoption costs. There was an overwhelming response as they sent in money and agreed to support us in prayer.

Six months later, we sent in our paperwork and started the long wait for permission to travel. As we waited, we read stories about other people's adoption experiences with older children. Our agency gave us permission to write to our new daughter and send her packages. We named her Amy. Every month, we sent her a letter and a package, hoping to show her how much we looked forward to having her in our family.

It was during these months that we decided one way to show our faith was to take a course in conversational Chinese. Here was another strange sounding language with yet a different alphabet. God gave us the gift we needed to learn enough of this strange language so we could communicate with Amy when she became our long sought-after daughter.

Finally, we received permission to travel. We were nervous, as some of the last adoption stories we had read were of older children who had second thoughts about their adoption and were consequently unhappy in the process. We felt we had prepared ourselves to embrace Amy into our hearts and home. We also prayed that Amy would be ready for us. We both prayed separately she would accept her new circumstances and family quickly and without regret. On the day we received her, she plopped down on the sofa next to us and said, " Hi, mom. Hi, dad." She has not looked back since.

DON AND DARLENE

The agency received a call concerning a six-year-old little boy from the streets of Houston that needed to be adopted. After prayer, we called two families to ask if they would pray about adopting this child. One of the families we called was Don and Darlene.

Later, Darlene told us they had prayed before going to bed, and then God woke her twice during the night. Both times, God told her, "I have a family for him, but it's not yours." The next morning, she dreaded calling to tell us what they felt God was saying, and before she was able to, we called her to say the other family had already called feeling God had told them that child was for them.

This, and many other, stories give us confidence that God truly is in control of "choosing" the "perfect" family for each child He places in a home.

THANKFULNESS TO GOD

Austin's verse Psalm 145 .
"The Lord is faithful to all his promises,
And loving toward all he has made.
The Lord upholds all those who fall
And lifts up all who are bowed down.
The eyes of all look to you,
And you give them their food at the proper time...
The Lord is righteous in all his ways
and loving toward all he has made.
The Lord is near to all who call on him,
to all who call on him in truth.
He fulfills the desires of those who fear him;
He hears their cry and saves them."

America's first Thanksgiving was set aside to celebrate the bounty that God had given the settlers in this country. They had a lot to be thankful for. How thankful are we on that last Thursday of November? Is it just a day off from work, a time to eat turkey, and watch football? Think about it. In the kitchen, aromas of the corn bread baking and the sage dressing in the turkey fill the air appetizingly as they sizzle there. That aroma is mixed with the sweet smell of the traditionally perfect pumpkin pie. The cranberries are bubbling on the stove. After such a day, we are more stuffed than the turkey. We join the cheers for our favorite football team as they trounce the opponents. All of this elicits fond memories. But at the end of the day, all is finished except for the leftovers. Thanksgiving will always be more than that for our family. Every day is thanksgiving for us.

We were taking advantage of the long holiday weekend by touring the capitol in Austin, Texas the day before Thanksgiving, 2004. Maybe pretending to be tourists would take our minds off our almost desperate desire to be parents. It was working. There was so much to see and learn on such a tour. Our time there was interrupted by *the* long- awaited phone call from the agency. A young woman who had made a plan to place her baby for adoption had chosen us. Thanksgiving will never be ordinary for us again.

Leading up to that memorable day were many of the same steps other couples had gone through. We researched until we found the right agency for us. We learned so much from their teaching at their annual orientation. We talked to other families who were in our situation. They helped us to feel better. The way the caseworkers talked about the adoption process in a practical hands-on way de-mystified the journey for us. Everyone related to the agency was a Christian. They were not afraid to talk about God's plan for babies to grow up in families with both moms and dads. We quickly put together a scrapbook and got our paperwork done so that birth mothers could begin looking at our profile.

A pregnancy takes nine months. That is how long we waited for *that* call. Have you ever told God to either do something to make your desire happen or to take away that desire? We admit to praying that one. He didn't take away the desire. He fulfilled it. I had prayed we would have a baby in 2004. Our baby was born on New Year's Eve of that year.

A few weeks after being chosen, we met both birth parents and some of their family members. God knit our hearts together. From the beginning, we fell in love with one another. We used the word "gracious" to describe how they responded to us. It didn't take long for us to be laughing like we had known each other forever. They brought a scrapbook with them they had made for us, complete with pregnancy pictures, ultrasound pictures, and letters for us. We learned our birth mom was a huge fan of the Texas Longhorns.

The name, Austin, is yet another amazing story. We thought we had come up with the perfect name for our son--one that honored our birth mother and reminded us of the joy we felt when we found out about him. Little did we know our birth mother and her mother had been thinking of names and had come up with the same exact name, during that same exact week. God is amazing!

When we met our birth father, we had an instant connection with him. His dad was an E.R. doctor like my husband. He was close to our age and reminded us of someone we would have "hung out" with. He was easy to talk to. We knew from the beginning our baby would have a rich heritage from both his birth parents.

At birth, the baby wasn't responding very well to stimuli. He was in an incubator at first and was being fed through a stomach tube. The next forty-eight hours were the longest "days" of our lives. We wanted to rush to the hospital to take care of him and talk to the doctors, but at this point we were not officially part of his family.

Our birth mom must have sensed our concern, because we finally got a call. She wanted us to come and help take care of him in the hospital. We couldn't have been happier. The birth family was at the hospital to meet, greet, and welcome us. That evening was so precious. Seven of us spent several hours together in the nursery while the nurse on duty turned a "blind" eye.

It took a little while for everything to sink in that night. It was not necessarily an instantaneous reality to be given a baby through adoption. It took a few hours or days for the realization to sink in that this was *our* baby. Forever. We took turns holding our son that night. We looked him all over from head to toe. I slowly realized he was beautiful, and he was ours now. It shook me to the depths of my soul to know this young mother had just given us a very real part of herself, to be ours, forever. And it was all happening at that moment. God was definitely in that room with us. Our birth mom wept and wept. Later, we found that her tears were because she was so happy to see her son with his "Daddy." We, too, had tears. Ours were for the goodness of God through this whole series of miracles.

All the baby needed was a little extra time for him to figure out his bottle. He stayed in the hospital for a week. We were there each morning to greet the doctor on her rounds and get updated on his progress. We were so glad that, as novice parents, we were given the opportunity to have a "go at it" in the setting of a hospital. There, the nurses could teach us everything we needed to know. That way we felt we couldn't mess up. Our birth mom came and visited several times, but it was becoming painful for her (in her grief) to be around her son. She knew she was not going to be able to take him home. She gradually detached herself, and we gradually attached ourselves. God was so gracious to give us that extra time to ease into being parents.

We took Austin home from the hospital to all our friends and family. We've never looked back. I will always express to our son that he is an extra-special gift. He has a wonderful story he can tell as he grows older. His is a story that is a picture of the way God adopts us into His family. He has a mommy and a daddy who love him very much. He also has a birth mom who loved him so much she made sure he had a daddy. Adoption was the only way she could provide that for him. God kept him safe and healthy so he could become our long-awaited son. We have so much to be thankful for.

So bring on the turkey and pumpkin pies; and join us for our continual Thanksgiving celebration.

GOD OVERCAME ADVERSITY

In the Old Testament, Jacob adopted his two
grandsons and blessed them right before he died.
The blessing was to give them a double share
of their father's inheritance. Here below is the
text that we put on Ellie's birth announcement
revised for a little girl!

"God, before whom our fathers Abraham and Isaac walked,
The God who has fed us all our lives long to this
day, the Angel who has redeemed us from all evil,
Bless this child; let our name be named upon her,
And the name of our fathers Abraham and Isaac;
And let her grow into a multitude in the midst of the
earth."

CARNIVAL: 1. The season just before Lent, marked by merrymaking
and feasting.
2. A traveling amusement show.

Almost everyone has memories of the thrill of riding a terrifying roller coaster and feeling his stomach rise in his throat. Or, a gentle Ferris wheel ride which lulled us into such peacefulness that we were reminded of another time long ago and far away. Or perhaps a ride on the horse on the Merry-go-round brings memories of our early childhood on a toy rocking horse, and we imagined we were galloping along with The Lone Ranger. The noises that surround us range from screams of happy passengers to rhythmic melodies of the sidewalk jazz musicians. The smells range from newly mown grass to popcorn and grilled hot dogs calling our name. These thoughts center around the county fair, Six Flags or even Disney World. Wherever the memory takes you, there is an element of adventure, intrigue, or even romance.

Our birth mom, with her one-year-old child was working and traveling with a carnival, when she found out she was pregnant again. Her boy friend had been such fun. Their time had been filled with adventure, but the romance was not serious. It was just superficial. Thus began a time that gave riding a roller coaster of life a whole new meaning.

With her first pregnancy, our birth mother had gone to Fatherheart Maternity Home for help. During her stay there, she had made the decision to parent her son. She knew adding a second baby would require more than she was able to give at this time in her life, but she wasn't sure if she was ready to place a baby for adoption. Adoption was so permanent. Could she live with that separation? She had a fairly good relationship with her boyfriend's mother. Maybe it would be easier if this woman were to raise the baby until she was better able to parent these two children on her own. She felt their relationship would grow, and she could visit her daughter occasionally, if not often. The idea seemed good at the time. Her next step was to see if this woman would be interested in parenting her grandchild.

The grandmother was excited about taking over the care of a newborn who had some of her genes, but she lived in England. Our birth mom just wasn't sure what to do. She started feeling a lot of pressure from her boyfriend and his parents to give her baby to them.

So our birth mom found herself in the airport, in her third trimester of pregnancy, about to board a plane to England and possibly give her baby to her boyfriend's parents to raise. Her mind was whirling. She started praying, right then and there, that God would show her what to do. If she wasn't supposed to go to England, would He make it very clear to her? Just then an announcement came, the plane was delayed. (That happens all the time. So what?) Then it was delayed again. With that second delay, our birth mom had a strong feeling God was answering her prayer. She didn't need any more of a sign than that. She ran out of the airport to the nearest phone. She called her close friend from the maternity home to ask for a place to stay until delivery.

The family in England did not just shrug their shoulders and say, "Okay." They talked a big talk about getting custody. But God, in His goodness, had other plans. Their lawyer was astute enough to explain to them that they would not get custody. If they fought the adoption, the birth mom would simply choose to parent. Although a few feathers were ruffled, they finally saw the wisdom in what their lawyer told them.

While staying with her friend from the maternity home, our birth mom prayed and agonized over the situation. She found it very difficult to even consider placing her baby for adoption. After much prayer and many discussions, she finally came to the conclusion God was directing her to place her baby with a strong Christian family. She began to look at family profiles and miraculously chose us to be the parents of her second child.

When we received the phone call from the agency, we were not expecting it at all. We were about to move to Germany in a few months. We had even considered withdrawing our profile from the agency. We knew if we adopted a baby, we would have to stay in the United States for six months until we could get a passport to bring the baby out of the country. We weren't sure how that would work. My husband had to report to work in Germany on August first. Only God knows why we hadn't just given up and stopped waiting for a baby. But He did know; He wanted us to wait for *this* baby.

I admit having some uncertainty about the birth dad's family, and about the fact that even if we did get this baby, I would be a single mom for approximately four months before we could take the baby out of the country and join my husband. I was very nervous, but God was still my Father and He had me right in the middle of His hand, where He wanted me. He didn't allow me to be tried or tested any more than I could bear. Because of all the hard times that came during those weeks, I learned a lot about trusting God. I also discovered something wonderful--I loved this baby intensely!

We actually met our birth mom in the beginning of April. We hadn't known what to expect. She seemed very sure about her decision to place her baby with us. Before we had met her, we hadn't known how much of an iron determination she really had. She *knew* that she needed to stay healthy for her baby, so she kept herself on a strict diet and didn't gain a lot of extra weight. She also *knew* she needed to finish school before delivery or she might never finish. She was working very hard and getting extra tutoring to make sure she could graduate. She *knew* she wanted us to be the parents of her baby from the first time she looked at our scrapbook profile. She never worried for a minute about the birth father. She *knew* in her heart he would never contest her decision to place the baby with us. Wow! We were so impressed that someone so young who had had such a hard life could understand so clearly what she needed to do. She even finished her high school requirements for graduation the day before delivery.

Placing her baby with our family was the hardest thing she had ever done, but our birth mother never wavered for a moment. She knew she had to say goodbye, but it was almost beyond her strength. While she was saying her goodbyes, we spent what seemed like hours waiting, in another building praying for her, and pacing back and forth. Finally, we were brought in and got to meet our daughter for the first time.

Although this was our second adoption, that experience did not make this one any easier. When I first saw our daughter, my thoughts were more with our birth mom than with the baby. I knew this baby was going to go home with us; there would be plenty of time to get to know her. For now my heart ached for the precious birth mother who would be going home empty-handed. The next several hours with our birth mom and her baby were bittersweet. We could feel her pain even as we felt our joy.

Our birth mom shared her hopes for her child's future achievements. She told us she wanted her to be able to do anything she wanted. Our birth mom had encountered all kinds of hurdles--all her life--and what she wanted most for this child was opportunity. . . the opportunity to do things she was never able to do herself. When the placement meeting was over, it was time to take a serious look at our baby. We wanted to memorize every part of her.

When placement was over we were walking in the clouds--so happy to have a daughter to raise with our son, so blessed, and so emotionally drained. We soon realized this poor birth mom was having a very hard time. Her depression over losing her child became a black cloud over her head. She couldn't see out. She was deep in grief. She knew she had made the right decision, but the physical and emotional pain was so great she didn't know where to turn. A machine-driven roller coaster ride was never like this.

We were so thankful for our friends at our adoption agency who were able to hold her hand through those first dark days. They showed her how her decision had given so many people great light. Gradually, she began to heal. Now after three years, I can say this birth mother is proud of what she did for her daughter. She still loves her child very much, and the pain she feels when she misses her is gradually being replaced by a great peace that can only come from God.

After only two months with our new daughter, Daddy had to go to Germany with the army. I stayed home parenting our two young children alone. Finalization was still four months away. We both found being apart difficult. My husband came back whenever he could, about once a month, and we talked to him daily on our computer's webcam. Through those four months I learned compassion for the many single moms who have no help. At least for me, I knew this experience was temporary.

Both children were so good as our things were packed up and sent to Germany. We even had to move in with a friend for a few weeks. It was a precious time for me to get to give so much extra attention to each child. Unnecessary distractions in our lives were stripped away as we waited for the court to finalize our second adoption. Our friends at the adoption agency were able to get the finalization court date on December sixth, EXACTLY six months after placement! That was truly a miracle. Even the passport came through on time without a hitch--another miracle. We were ready to fly to Germany to start our new life there.

I always want our daughter to know what a miracle she is. She is not only the miracle of life, born healthy and normal, but she is also the miracle that is adoption. She is not only our daughter, but someone else calls her daughter as well. She is a precious pearl – a gem that God formed out of great trouble and adversity.

People might try to tell her that the beginning of her life, her conception, was not beautiful and wonderful. But her daddy and I believe EVERY conception is beautiful and wonderful. Her life is a miracle. God made her into a beautiful baby who will bring light into the lives of many people.

It may seem we went through a lot to get our baby girl. But it was worth every second, every hurdle, and every lesson learned. We are so thankful God gave us our two beautiful children. They have made our lives so happy with their sweet smiles and hugs and kisses. We will never forget each child is truly a MIRACLE.

The roller coaster ride is not exactly a walk in the park for our birth mom. But her body and her emotions are gradually reaching a balance—another mark of God's miracle work in her.

HAND OF GOD
SUZIE

Psalm 139:15-18

My frame was not hidden from you
When I was made in the secret place.
When I was woven together in the depths of the earth,

Your eyes saw my unformed body.
All the days ordained for me
Were written in your book
Before one of them came to be.

How precious to me are your thoughts, O God!
How vast is the sum of them!

Were I to count them,
They would outnumber the grains of sand.
When I awake,
I am still with you.

Elizabeth had placed Ellie, our first daughter, in a family with a mom, and a doctor-dad, and an older brother, two and a half years before her second daughter, Moriah, was born. It seemed natural for her to place Moriah with the same family.

When Moriah, later to be called Suzie, was born with some damage to her hands and right toes from Amniotic Band Syndrome, Elizabeth wondered if the family would reject her daughter because she was not "perfect." She insisted that many pictures be sent to the couple ahead of their long trip to Texas to consummate the adoption. She wanted no surprises when they saw her hands and foot.

The pictures were sent. When the call came from this dad (after they had viewed the pictures), his heart was beautifully evident in his words.

He said, "Yes, we saw the hands and foot, but I can't take my eyes off her beautiful face."

Her new mom expressed these words to Suzie. "Your Daddy and I will do everything in our power to give you hands that are fixed, but I want you to know, whatever the outcome of the surgeries ahead… ultimately, God gave you your hands because he knew they would glorify Him just the way they are. He made no mistake when He crafted each part of you. Your Daddy and I believe every single part of you is beautiful. The Bible says, 'How beautiful are the feet of those who bring good news.'   You will be bold with your testimony, carrying the Good News to all you meet. I see God using you as his messenger, not in spite of these hands and feet, but because of them. I know that your hands, when they serve God, will be perfect and will give God EVEN GREATER praise than hands that were born like everyone else's!

"I don't know what your future looks like, baby girl, but I am confident that future is blazingly bright. My vision of your future is of hands that may look a little different than other people's, but of hands that laugh at the notion of "disability." I have a vision of you playing on a playground, swinging on the monkey bars with both hands. I see your hands turning the pages of your Bible as you learn to read it on your own. I have a vision of your right hand shaking the hand of the principal of your high school and of the president of your college, as you walk by with a diploma. I see you typing at a computer and playing the piano. I have a vision of a ring placed on the fourth finger of your left hand, and of a husband who loves you through and through inside and out. I have a vision of busy hands that raise babies and grandbabies. And I know that the God who rules the universe truly cares about you and will give you a brighter future than even I can't imagine.

"We don't know why God made your hands and feet the way he did, but we know that he loves you and so do we. We can't wait to take care of you and help your hands and feet to serve God.

"God makes his glory and grace known in many ways, but one of the most startling is through our troubles and problems. He says that his strength is perfected in our weaknesses. I know that you will be able to show the world how great our God is through your weaknesses.

"I want you to know that your birth mother, Elizabeth, loves you very, VERY much. She says that you are perfect and beautiful. Placing you with our family is an act of sacrificial love, and I think an act of worship too. I know that she wants you to remember that. I love you as much as

Elizabeth does. She knows that this is the right decision for you, and she wants you to know that she loves you exactly the way God made you. Her love for you is sacrificial because she longs for you to have a Daddy and the kind of life she never had."

WALKING IN THE FOOTSTEPS OF JESUS

Just inside the door of our home are ten sets of shoes. Until just over seven yeas ago, you would have seen only five pair. That was when adoption miracles began in our family. These shoes are a unique as the feet of their owners. The descriptions will give you a clear picture o the members of our family.

Dad Dennis' shoes are sturdy leather flip-flops with fake fur inside: tough, strong, no-frills, but soft and inviting inside. They are comfortable and calming and keep him relaxed in demanding situations.

Gabe (18) wears funky European loafers that will carry him through high school graduation this Spring to Norway for a year of extreme sports and language development, then perhaps West Point or something similar. We delight and grieve over this next step.

Elias (16) covers his feet with black/white, cool/comfortable Sambas. They take him out driving to his widespread gatherings with friends and match the piano where he plays complex improvisational pieces every day. They are the only shoes he'll take on his trip to Ethiopian orphanages and clinics in February.

Magdalene (13) wears plaid high-healed wedges that are tough enough to let her cart around a sibling on her hip and still feel stylish. She is a joy and now has fallen in love with the Ethiopian people.

Malachi (7) does everything enthusiastically. His rubber boots with handles are the best. He can race out the door without stopping except to grab a little sibling for whom he is always available. He calls Ezra his "Little Chocolate Kiss."

Salome (4) prefers furry, cheetah-patterned ballet slippers, rain or shine. She loves what she loves. Purses, lip-gloss, fingernail polish, and gum are her favorite accessories. She often passionately exclaikms, "We all love each other!"

Zion (almost 2) matches Malachi and is always ready to "GO GO!" He is tough and tender, competitor to the extreme with new brother Emmaus, who he alls simply, "Guy!" (very loudly.)

Emmaus Kibrom (2 ½) places his brown Converse tennis shoes in a perfect line, just beside Mommy's fake snake-skin clogs. Since the clogs are the first shoes he saw on me, they are the ones I should wear! His bowl, spoon, jacket, clothes and "Gold Bug Book" must stay precisely as he wants them. This complex, bright, exquisite boy is our sweet blossom, opening slowly and sometimes painfully.

Ezra Bethlehem (1), just learning to walk, lights up a room with her smile. She softens her young brothers' competitive spirits as she pads around unobstrusively on leather-soled pink shoes. Her gentle patience is a balm to our extreme days.

Our precious new babies journeyed home October 2, accompanied by Dennis, Gabriel, and Magdalene. The joy and grief of the footsteps of the Ethiopian people humble and amaze us. The brave path taken by each of our new birth mothers is a stunning example of the strength God gives to the most selfless in our world. Gabriel's words most effectively describe the way he, Dennis, and Mags observed the beautiful people of Ethiopia.

"And what people, the street urchins, the business men, the beautifully unique and strikingly different from any race I had seen. Their skin, although dark, was not ashen, but mostly a rich honey tone. Their faces each showed a small nose, a soft, less pronounced jar, and poignant, piercing eyes of Ethiopia. Loving but hard, tender but indifferent, resilient to pain and familiar with suffering."

No matter the size, shape or color of the shoes, each step our family takes is following in the footsteps of Jesus. God brought our family together one miracle at a time; and wherever He leads us from here, we will follow.

AMAZING GRACE

"Receive and experience the amazing grace of the Master,
Jesus Christ, deep, deep within yourselves." Philippians 4:23

"Pure grace and nothing but grace be with all who love our
Master, Jesus Christ." Ephesians 6:24

"The amazing grace of the Master, Jesus Christ, the
extravagant love of God, the intimate friendship of the Holy
Spirit, be with all of you." 2 Corinthians 13:14

Our miracle story begins with, and ends with, "Amazing Grace." Although all of us experience miracles in our lives every day, some miracles tend to cast light into our daily routine of shadows, while others tend to shine a light so bright and pure that shadows simply do not exist. It is about the latter we are excited, and it is with humility we share our testimony of God's amazing grace, hoping to honor Him with glory and praise.

I begin our story with a miracle of healing. At the age of seventeen my wife to be contracted viral encephalitis and was not expected to live. The doctors said if she did survive she would not possess any quality of life. At this hour of darkness, when the doctors counseled the family to plan for the worst, God had other plans for this young lady. He not only healed her, but He also strengthened a community through her illness. She was completely cured by His healing and remains very healthy to this day.

Our story continued to unfold as God united north and south, then east and west by bringing two young people together. I was born in Michigan, but I got to Texas as soon as I could. It was then we met on a blind date. Yes, it was the "fourth of July" in September that year. It was rather like "love at first sight." However, soon after, she was temporarily assigned to California, and I was exploring a job in Switzerland. God quickly settled all this. We married.

God's plan was working so well we decided to help Him customize it for us. We set out to plan our careers, to plan when we would start our

46

family, even to plan the composition of our family - one boy and one girl. Yes, we planned our lives so well that we got to experience several years of unexplained non-success. This included several years with infertility specialists, a failed private adoption, a roadblock of time for foreign adoption, and the highest of hopes and the lowest of disappointments along the way.

Doctors told us we could not biologically have children. Our dreams were shattered. We were exhausted, physically and emotionally drained; our hearts were bruised by every news story of wasted children, and we seemed at another dark hour.

We were resolved to a life without children. We were distraught and broken from our plan, yet God's plan was very much intact. So we rested in the stillness of the dark and listened. We then realized we had forgotten to include God in our plan. In the silence, we started learning sign language at our church. We were preparing to sign the Christmas pageant, " When Love Came Down".

It was then God sent to us three very special angels. The first two were a mother and her daughter. This mom was in our sign class preparing for the pageant. Her daughter came to one of the practices. While we commented to the mom about her daughter's beauty and sweet disposition, the mom told us this gift came down to them through a small Christian adoption agency. Later, we met God's third angel in the form of the husband of the woman, the dad of this beautiful little girl.

This couple told us their story. They had four children, all adopted from the small Christian agency. Intrigued by seemingly perfect success, we were cautiously optimistic for fear of another disappointment. They told us that they were speaking at an orientation coming up in March and encouraged us to sign up. We did.

Soon the March orientation arrived. An absolutely perfect day started with meeting new friends. We shared laughter and tears. We listened to birth mothers, adoptive parents, adopted children, and the agency's staff. Each shared testimonies of God's work. We simply fell in love with everyone. It was easy to see this was where God wanted us to be. We felt totally inadequate. There were so many great couples in search of God's children. We were told to start praying for our birth mother now. We did.

As we left that day, we felt an excitement much like the newness of the coming of spring. Yet we were optimistically cautious. The Christmas pageant, "When Love Came Down," incited me to predict a miracle. I said, "We will have a baby by Christmas." My wife cautioned, "Honey, I really hope you don't get your hopes up . . ." I interrupted, "We will have a baby by Christmas."

Our story would now reveal the miracle of patience, which was truly God's patience with us. We started gathering documents. The home study process began. The financial commitment required a shift in priorities. We began to picture a lifestyle change. The creation of a scrapbook depicting our life now seemed challenging. It also seemed appropriate for my wife to have a heart to heart talk with God. Although it may have seemed somewhat like an ultimatum, her surrender speech went something like this, "Lord, I am willing to go down this path with You again, but at the end of this journey, I am done. Either we have a baby or it's a closure. One way or the other, I have to let this be over."

As summer came, my wife was faced with the task of creating a scrapbook representing the totality of our lives. The creative talents of many friends, family members, and the grace of God made it happen. I could only help technically as I am a color-blind engineer. Alas, the scrapbook, much like an award winning recipe submitted to the state fair, was completed in August, hand-delivered, and placed before the "judges". We were told to continue to pray and wait. We did.

Our wait was not long, for in October an agency worker called us and said, "I have a situation I need you to pray about. A young woman has chosen you to be her daughter's parents." Wow! What a miracle! And, pray we did. We called the agency worker back in a few days and said, "We know this is God's will." We had been praying for our birth mom since the March orientation, even though we didn't know her name.

Our quest seemed to be nearing a successful conclusion, but it was only the beginning. When we met the birth mother for the first time, we were all very nervous. As the jitters settled down, it was easy to see a very strong, determined young woman who unselfishly wanted the absolute best for her daughter. She wanted to give her daughter what she had and cherished when she was growing up. Her gift would be that which she could not provide at this point in her life--a mother and a father to raise such a precious gift from God. We very simply fell in love with this young woman, and God's plan continued to unfold. Minutes turned to hours as we laughed, cried, and developed a new bond. This joy led us to reaffirm our covenant with each other, as well as our covenant with God.

The calendar neared Thanksgiving and our birth mom asked if we would agree to a second meeting because her family would be visiting from

California. We anxiously agreed, excited and honored to meet her parents and two brothers. We did meet her family the day after Thanksgiving. We thoroughly enjoyed spending time with our new extended family. It was amazing how similar our families were. It was amazing how our broken roads had led us back to His plan. On December 18, 2003, "Love" came down in the form of an amazing little angel. She became the first grandchild on the three sides of these families. Two days later, on December 20th, (my birthday) we brought our baby home. She was introduced to an arrival party of about forty very excited friends and family members. Indeed, it was an amazing birthday for me.

Baby Gracen is now seven years old and an amazing little girl. She has become the air we breathe, the the pulse of our beating hearts, and the "Amazing Grace" of our awesome God above. She is a constant reminder that we can never fall or climb farther than God's "Amazing Grace" can reach.

MOTHER'S DAY

"Yes, the Lord has done amazing things for us. What Joy!"
Psalm 126:3

This Mothers' Day as I sat in the quiet of the morning contemplating my children, I was overwhelmed at the extraordinary way I was blessed to celebrate this day. This year I was celebrating my motherhood of four children with two adopted children, our birth child and a foster child. Actually, this was the second year that Mother's Day had happened this way, but this year was even more joyful as we anticipated the up-coming adoption of our foster son. Reminiscing over my dreams of motherhood as a girl, I remembered always wanting four children, a red head, and the opportunity to raise both boys and girls. I was the oldest of four (three sisters and a brother) and I had red hair. So those had been my dreams. Looking at my children now I marvel at the miraculous ways God has brought them into our lives. Each has a very special story.

Keith and I married when we were in our thirties following a military career for him and a career in foreign missions for me. In fact, as I left the states for the third time to serve overseas, this time as a career missionary, I was approaching my thirtieth birthday, and I was at peace with my singleness (though I had made no secret about my desires to marry and to have a family one day). I arrived in the Gaza Strip in late September, and at the end of October, Keith was transferred to Gaza from Northern Israel. The story of God's arrangement to bring us together is a miracle in itself. It could only have come about by His hand orchestrating the entire situation. Four years later, we were married, as God led both of us to retire from our respective careers. Being a little older, we were eager to begin our family.

The next part of our story was much like many others as we stepped through the hoops on our own journey to begin a family. After more than a year of surgeries, procedures, medications, and a multitude of visits to a fertility doctor, we were told we should look at other options. We really had no chance of becoming pregnant. In a state of shock and disappointment, we began to pray and wait for God's timing on pursuing adoption. The best that came about as we waited was that God connected us with Loving Alternative. Their heart is for ministry to all sides of the adoption triangle. Working with them encouraged us.

Early that January, we learned a birth mother had chosen us. We met her and the paternal grandparents. At this time the birth father was not around. The miracle of "Deena" coming to us had begun. Our adoption caseworker had made us aware that no matter how committed birth mothers are to placing their children for adoption, once their babies are born, they really have to make the decision all over again. Well, we heard that but didn't really expect a problem because Hannah had seemed so "sure'" about her decision to place her baby.

However, after birth, Hannah and Chuck wanted to take Deena back to the grandparents' house and be with her a few days. We were told this was not a good sign but we had no way to stop it. Deena went home with her birth mom. She had been born on a Tuesday, and we had been scheduled to pick her up the following Sunday. However, late Saturday evening, we got word that they had changed their minds. We were devastated! We immediately called our parents and siblings and asked them to pray with us. I distinctly remember one of Keith's sisters saying "I'm going to pray Chuck does something that makes Hannah realize parenting is not easy and gives her a picture of what his involvement would really be like." Well, that is exactly what happened! He was out all night, and by morning, Hannah was having second thoughts.

Because it was so "iffy," we thought the best place for us to be was at church that Sunday. That is when the call came through for us to get to the adoption agency as fast as we could. We arrived to experience the most joyful, and yet emotionally wrenching, day of our lives. The whole birth family was there to say "goodbye" to this precious little girl. They placed her in Keith's arms. It was gut wrenching. As all adoptive parents can attest, the day of placement is one of indescribable joy for the new adoptive family, but one of deepest grief for the birth parents. As the ones experiencing the joy, and observing the pain, it is a unique and unusual experience. The agency calls it "bitter sweet."

Thus began our wonderful journey as parents. Four and a half months later, we found out we were pregnant with Nikki. Anyone who has had a newborn in the house knows the last thing on your mind is adding to your family, but God had set another plan in motion. When we saw the test was positive, the first words out of our mouths were "God meant for us to have Deena." We felt if we had become pregnant any sooner, we would not have pursued adoption at the same time, and Deena would not have been have become our daughter. God's timing is always so amazing to us.

When Deena was thirteen months old, Nikki joined our family with a head full of red hair! According to the doctor and all the medical tests, we should never have been able to conceive a child. God was gracious and gifted us with that special experience, but not until His adoption plan was set in motion.

In the meantime Hannah and Chuck had two more boy children. We were contacted about adopting them. As God would have it, Hannah and Chuck were reunited at the birth of their second son. They made plans to parent and become a family. They moved to a northern Midwestern state. We were not to parent these two boys.

A few months later Hannah became pregnant again. They knew that once the baby was born, the boys and the baby would be taken into the custody of Child Protective Services in that northern state. This motivated Hannah to return to the relative safety of Texas to deliver this child.

We knew nothing about their arrival in Texas until just a couple of days before Anna was born. At that point, all we knew to do was to pray that God would rescue this precious life. Less than one week after learning they were in Texas, we were making plans to add another little girl to our family. Our little firecracker was born on July Fourth. We brought her home six days later. Deena and Anna were full sisters. God gave them each the special gift of getting to grow up together.

God had increased our faith with all of the miraculous ways He had answered our prayers. So during the next four years, we continued to wait and to pray about how He was going to add that fourth child to our family. Shortly after getting Anna, we learned we were pregnant again and were ecstatic. So this was God's answer to how He would add to our family. However, we soon faced the pain and loss of a miscarriage. So we began waiting and trusting yet again for God's plan to unfold.

Our collective faith continued to grow. When the opportunity came to help out Little Footprints Ministry, near our area, by fostering children, we couldn't wait to get involved. The first possibility was two small brothers who were in CPS custody. That turned out to be quite sticky with relatives and birth fathers involved. The courts made a decision that did not include us.

The next chance was for an eighteen-month-old boy named Robert. They anticipated he would soon become adoptable. At the same time a newborn would be leaving the hospital in the care of Little Footprints. He needed to go to a licensed foster home. Would we consider fostering him as well. Of course in our hearts we wanted to love them all. In reality we knew we could not add a newborn and a toddler to our home all at once. We told the director we would take either child, but they needed to decide which one they needed for us to take. Four days later, the director called to say they felt Malachi, the newborn, was to come live with us as a foster child. (Robert, the 18-month-old went to live with relatives.) We picked him up that night. We have found along the journey, God has kept our hearts ever ready for the children He would give us. Sometimes they came quickly, before we had everything "in place" for their arrival.

Fostering was a new experience for us. Malachi's birth mom was planning to work with CPS so she could eventually parent him. We were not anticipating what God was planning.

Picture this "web" of circumstances during our fostering period: Malachi's older half sister, Susie, had been placed with one family. We had been foster parenting Malachi since his birth. (The idea in adoption of siblings is to keep them together whenever possible, like Deena and Anna.) Malachi's birth mom got pregnant a third time, (Levi) with no chance of parenting any of them. God stepped in and untangled it to everyone's satisfaction and best interest. Levi was placed into the family who had adopted Susie, and Malachi was released to be adopted by us.

Six months later the other foster family and we were standing together before the same judge who had previously granted the adoption of Susie. We both added a fourth child to our families that day. Malachi and Levi were officially adopted with their brothers and sisters looking on. What a special day for our two families to celebrate together as we adopted these precious brothers, both of whom God had so lovingly placed in our lives.

Only twelve years have passed since we adopted our first precious daughter, and God has done exceedingly abundantly more than we ever dreamed or imagined in giving us a family. Not only were we blessed with experiencing God's amazing miracle of birth, but we were also privileged to share in the wonderful love and sacrifice of adoption. Finally, we were taken on the journey of foster parenting as God fulfilled our desires of a fourth child, a son.

God always gives over-abundantly. Each time I sit back and survey our quiver, be it once or a dozen times a day, I can't help but smile.

Yes, the Lord has done amazing things for us! What Joy! Psalm 126:3

JIM AND CAROL

Never has a movie, or a life experience, impacted me like *The Blind Side* did when I saw it a few weeks ago. I cried through the whole movie. It was a wonderful story of a life and family changed. But I cried for very different reasons than most might think. I didn't cry because the boy found a family. I didn't even cry because his life was transformed. I cried because I have forgotten to appreciate how GOD has put our family together. I think my family and the Touhys only have one thing in common--GOD created it. Jim and I never set out to change the life of a child. We started this process of creating a family being very selfish; we wanted children. We did not go to Loving Alternative and say "we want to change the world's view of transracial families" or "we want to be in vogue with Hollywood." We were open to whatever GOD wanted for us. And for that I am eternally grateful. But I have forgotten to be thankful for my children as I swim in clutter of dinner, laundry, making beds, wiping noses, and cleaning up spilt milk. The movie reminded me that MY life has been changed by my children and if theirs is changed, then it is only a byproduct of my love for them. So today I am thankful, grateful and appreciative of what I have in Jesus and in whom my family is. If you see this movie, and I hope you do, remember that keeping an open heart can change your life.

Tiffini, age 9, is more than 4 ½ feet tall. She is an amazing reader and you find her either in a pet shop with a toy or sitting with book in her hand. She wants to be a teacher when she grows up. She spends lots of time trying to get Will to be still and listen as she goes over his colors with him. She is so precious and loving. If she were a chocolate candy, she would be a 3 Musketeer; yummy on the outside and soft on the inside.

Anna, age 7, is 4 feet tall. She is a lean, mean fighting machine. She is full of passion for whatever she is doing. She hates to lose at anything and is just learning to read, but math is her thing. She loves matchbox cars and playing pet shop with her sister. She will be an amazing athlete when she gets older as she is very coordinated. If she were chocolate candy, she would be a Snickers: luscious on the outside and a mixture of soft, crunchy on the inside.

Will, age 4, is forty-four inches tall and sixty-three pounds. He is large for a five-year-old and he is only four. He is so sweet; we call him the gentle giant. He is, however, all BOY. He is all about the "ball" and things that move. He asked for a motorcycle for Christmas—needless to say, he did not get one. If he were chocolate candy, he would be M & M's; you reach in one time and get red and blue, then the next time you get green and brown. Whether it is the mini size or the one-pound bag, you really don't want to shop short of finishing them all.

We are "beyond" blessed at what God has given us in this family.

BLESSINGS THROUGH PAIN

"Why are you downcast, O my soul? Why so disturbed within me?

Put your hope in God, for I will yet praise him, My Savior and my God." Psalm 42:5

"Here am I, and the children God has given me." Hebrews 2:13 b

There are many events in our lives that take place and we are hard pressed to find the reason for them. We look back and speculate, "Perhaps I went through that in order to meet so and so or to do such and such..." We wonder what lesson we learned or what great attribute was cultivated in us. The truth is, we will never know the full extent or the importance of such events until we are no longer in this life. On this side of heaven the extreme complexity of it all would be too mind-boggling for us to comprehend. Not knowing exactly who, what, when, where, and why in our lives creates in us a God-made void only He can fill. He wants us to turn to Him for our answers and to accept that He only tells us what we need to know and that it is for our own good.

We had been matched. We had met with a very pregnant young lady who wanted us to adopt her son as soon as he was born. Everyone, including the caseworkers, the counselors, our family and even the birth mother, it seemed, was excited and positive about this. We had no reason to think otherwise. We were introduced to the birth mother in September, and a healthy baby boy arrived at the end of November. We were parents for five days. For five days we had a son whom we were blessed to have—even for such a short time. He touched our lives in ways he will never know. He was not meant to stay with us though; God had another plan for him. We thought God must be mistaken and there had been a great misunderstanding. Why did this happen? Why were we allowed to bring this child home and to care for him, only to have him taken away? Why? We were heartbroken and confused. Everyone, including the birth mother had said it was God's plan for us to parent the little boy. However, for reasons we still don't understand, the birth mother changed her mind about the adoption plan we had all set in motion. We had to give the baby boy back to her. Never before or since has this happened in this agency.

It was one of the worst days of our lives. We just knew she was making a mistake and in the process, she was breaking our hearts. But God was gracious enough to surround us with supportive family, church family, and friends who lifted us up through that dark time. We grew closer to each other as a couple and gained great new insights about just how much God loved us. We became more confident that God still had something great in store for us.

In mid-January, we received a phone call from our adoption agency asking if we wanted to come get a baby boy...tomorrow! He was one day old, and the birth mother had picked us out a few weeks prior to his birth. The adoption agency had chosen to save us from the emotional roller coaster ride by not calling us earlier in the process. We prayed and knew we had to be willing to put our fragile hearts on the line if we wanted to be parents again. So we called the agency back and told them, "Yes." We both thought we would be guarded and somewhat distant from the baby at first, but as soon as we laid our eyes on him, we knew he was our son forever. God had blessed us in an amazing way. We found the joy of the Lord in our sorrows, and He gave us the desire of our hearts. How great is His faithfulness!

In March of that same year we discovered we were pregnant. What a shock! We had a two month old and felt in our hearts our lives were complete. We thought our cups were "filled to overflowing," but boy, oh boy, were we surprised at how full they could become. At Christmas, our house had two baby boys. Our adoption journey had been full of surprises, wonder, grief, and joy.

Tonight, our son through adoption, gave us a kiss goodnight. As we said our prayers together, we thought for the millionth time, "How awesome you are God." God knew this boy would fulfill the need we had to be parents and he would bring us so much joy.

Our son is blessed because his birth mother prayed for him while he was in her womb, and she thought about him and what kind of life she wanted him to have. In what, to us, is one of the most unselfish acts of love, she created a plan of adoption for him. She realized the environment in which she lived would not be the best for him. She looked for a couple who would love this boy very much and give him the life she would have wanted to give him if she could have. She made the hardest decision of her life, and in so doing, she altered the course of many lives. We will forever be grateful to her and to God for allowing us to be his parents. We can't imagine all that went into orchestrating this event--this miracle. All we know is we feel blessed beyond measure. We are reminded of God's faithfulness and His might every time we look at the children God has placed in our care.

OUR GIFT FROM GOD

"You will be sorrowful, but your sorrow will be turned into joy." John 16:20.

"Mary, grab the other phone! It's Doris from Loving Alternative."
It was the "call" every prospective couple waits to get.

"John and Mary, I'm so glad you are both home. You have been chosen by one of our birth moms to adopt her baby. After I tell you all about her and the baby she carries, you will have the opportunity to pray and to see if God confirms what Sally feels is the right decision. Then you can call me in the next couple of days with your answer."

After hearing all the details and hanging up the phone, I whispered through my joyful tears, "John, after that last miscarriage, I had just about given up hope that we'd ever be parents. Even this call seems like a miracle. Let's pray right now."

It had always been our desire to have children. We had never dreamed we would have problems having our own. I had thought I would birth two children and then adopt two children. I had always wanted to adopt because I knew there were children who deserved a loving home. After eleven years of marriage, though, we still were not able to have children, but we continued to believe God. A visit to the doctor showed fibroid cysts in my uterus. Due to the size of them, he said they were the reason I was not able to conceive. Once the fibroids were removed surgically, we expected I would be able to conceive. We were very hopeful, but I still didn't get pregnant.

My doctor suggested we go to a fertility doctor. We set up the appointment. We were very excited. This doctor said, "Based on past medical problems and age, I won't be able to help you." That was a very disappointing day. We were very discouraged and disheartened. Again, God gave us the strength to move on.

We still believed God would perform a miracle, and I would get pregnant. The next year I became very sick, and the doctors had to perform a hysterectomy. It was so amazing. God gave us a great peace in the midst of this situation.

A friend suggested we adopt. I was very open to the idea since I had always planned to adopt. Their story was very encouraging. They had adopted within three months of starting the process. I was excited. Even though I had heard adoption of infants could take a while, I believed for ours to be quick. We started the process in 2004 by completing the application and questionnaire. We went to an orientation in March of 2005. Now we were ready. 2005 . . . nothing. In 2006, we had some prospects. In these particular cases, there were some special situations. The agency needed to verify if it was okay with us to show our family profile to the birth mom. I didn't want to get my hopes up, so I tried to remain low key. In both cases, we were not chosen. This was very hard.

In 2007, nothing happened. We would receive the newsletters from our adoption agency of the adoptions that had occurred. I was happy for the other couples, but it was also very painful. I asked my husband, "What is wrong with us?" I thought maybe it was because I was over forty years old. I told God if He didn't want us to have children to please remove the desire from within our hearts. How many just such prayers has God heard over the years?

We had waited four years for "the call" from Loving Alternative. Three years into our wait, we accepted the informal care of our niece's baby Savanna. Our niece was deployed overseas. When she returned, she would claim her child. Savanna came to live with us when she was six weeks old. This only increased our desire to have children. We taught her to call us "Auntie" and "Uncle." At this time, she did not understand who we were. I think our decision about our titles was really for our emotional protection. We held and loved this baby girl for fourteen months. We hoped that by some miracle, Savanna's time with us would not end.

It was getting close to the time for our niece to return and to take her daughter. When Savanna was about twelve months old, we received that long-awaited call from our adoption agency. My husband called me at work and said the adoption agency had just called. I assumed they were calling to see how we were doing. We called back. The agency worker asked if we were still interested in adopting. We said, "Of course." She said a mother had chosen us as the adoptive parents. (My eyes are tearing up even now as I write this. That was such a very special day.) I expected her to say she would deliver in one or two months, but she said the baby was two weeks old. WOW! I couldn't believe my ears. I felt numb. Then she said we could possibly have the baby placed in our home within two weeks. A double WOW! Now my head was spinning. I was so excited. I wanted to SHOUT, "THANK YOU, LORD."

We had to get all our paperwork current. At the time, my husband's parents were living with us. They had to be interviewed and have background checks. The clearance reports had been taking a long time. They indicated this could be a slow down in the process. I told them my Father God would take care of it. And He did. They had an unusually fast turnaround.

We first got to see our son in his foster home on our 20th Wedding Anniversary. That was the best gift we could ever have given to each other. When I saw him, I still couldn't believe he was going to be our son. He was so precious and peaceful. He was a beautiful baby. We had to decide on a name. My husband picked his first name; it means "Gift of God."

The day finally came for us to pick up our son. I think I was still in shock because I had not cried until he was placed in my arms. It finally hit me. He is really ours. What an Awesome God we serve. God has definitely blessed us with a miracle, and we are so very grateful for our "Gift of God."

No child can replace another; but Nathaniel is loved and fits right into the empty arms left by Savanna's departure. We are calling God's timing and plan nothing but a pure miracle.

MARYEMMA'S STORY

"The Lord your God is with you He is mighty to save. He will take great delight in you; He will quiet you with His love. He will rejoice over you with singing." Zephaniah 3:17

At the beginning of our story, my husband was pastor of a church, and I was working as an assistant manager at a local motor bank. I had just completed my degree in photography, and my husband was working on his Masters of Divinity degree at a seminary, three hours from our home.

Before we had children or knew the "ins and outs" of adoption, we "fell" into a situation that whetted our appetites to becoming parents. Through a strange set of circumstances, we found ourselves caring for a baby girl in our home. In a way, we were baby sitting 24/7. Communication with the birth mom was through a third party. Much was lost in the translation, as they say. It got to the point that we knew we'd better find legal counsel. We couldn't find a lawyer who would take the case; but we were directed to a local adoption ministry.

That was where our education about adoption began. They were very gracious in giving us information about birth mothers and their needs, and we learned how to legally and safely walk through an adoption. Soon we realized this baby was not meant to join our family. I cried and loved on that baby, and we prayed and prayed and prayed. Finally, the day came when the baby's mother came and took her back. Again we cried and prayed, but we had to let her go. We heard her mother is raising her now and doing a good job, and we heard she is happy and healthy.

After this traumatic event, we called the worker at the adoption ministry to let her know what had happened. As she prayed with us over the phone, our shattered emotions began to heal. She said they had an orientation coming up in March, and if we were interested, we would need to get our initial paperwork filled out. We did.

During the March orientation, we fell in love with all the different facets of this adoption ministry. Our hearts had always been drawn to young women who were pregnant, unwed, alone, and hurting. It seemed natural for us to be drawn into this ministry.

The next step was for us to complete the home study. The caseworker and we began an unusually sweet relationship during the interview sessions, and she began to share prayer needs with us. One of the needs was for a little baby girl and her young mother. The baby had been born on March 12, 2003, to a young woman who said she had not realized she was pregnant. This birth mother was not prepared to be a mother and was confused about her situation.

However, she seemed very wise about what she wanted for her daughter. She knew enough to ask a nurse about adoption. The nurse contacted our agency, and they helped this birth mother walk through this life-changing decision. The baby was placed with a wonderful foster family while the ladies at the agency developed a relationship with her birth mother. The birth dad's rights had to be terminated, as well as the birth mom's. In this case there was a definite need for godly intervention.

The birth dad didn't even know he'd fathered a child until a letter came, followed by a visit from the adoption staff. They asked if he would be willing to waive his rights to parent the baby, but he was mad and determined not to give up his rights easily.

Being pastors, we have lots of opportunities to pray for all kinds of situations. This one was added to our list, and we prayed especially for the welfare of the baby.

We had met the Loving Alternatives' staff in February of that year. They had no "waiting list," so we had no idea how long our wait would be until we could become "proud parents." However, we had *our* "scheduled" goals. We were doing *our* thing. . . God's way.

The morning before we received "the call" from the agency, I was offered a managerial position, which I agreed to take. At noon, just before lunch break, my phone rang. It was the adoption caseworker who said she had some important information. There was a baby they wanted us to pray about adopting. I was floored! I left work a couple of hours early that day, and my husband and I met with the adoption staff. The baby they wanted us to adopt was the very one we had been praying for these last few months! We had been praying for this baby, for someone else. The baby was now almost four months old. The baby's birth father had finally realized he would not be able to parent her. He had signed away his rights. We were in awe. We laughed and cried and prayed and praised God.

The next few days passed in a blur of praising God. Everything we needed for a newborn came from family, church folks, and co-workers. I had always wanted to stay home with our babies. This meant quitting my new job. My boss rejoiced with us and worked it out so I could use my two weeks notice as vacation time. The bank gave me two weeks extra pay as a baby gift. I was immediately free to be a mother! God had to be laughing at our elation and surprise. He always gives us praiseworthy gifts. And when He gives us good things, He makes sure they are "out-of-this-world" good. There is no way the whole process of bringing her home to our family was anything other than the holy handiwork of Almighty God. July 14, 2003, we became the proud parents of four-months-old, thirteen pound, eleven ounce, twenty-five inches long, beautiful baby girl.

We never got to meet our daughter's birth mother, but we did receive a sweet letter from her, and we were able to write a letter to her. She will be forever in our hearts, and we praise God for her. Our family and friends and church welcomed our daughter with loads of love and lots of prayers of praise. I have never experienced God's hand moving in such an amazing act of strength as I did during the process of making us a family. We enjoyed our supervision visits with the agency's staff. The foster family who loved and cared for our daughter her first four months have become dear close friends of ours. She was their first foster baby, and that made her very special to them. They wanted to have a life-long relationship with her and her forever family. God is doing just that.

Our daughter is seven now and is a funny, witty, imaginative, creative, and high energy little girl. She is just like her daddy in that she never meets a stranger, loves to talk to people, makes new friends daily, and has a crazy hysterical sense of humor. She is like me in that she likes to have things planned out, loves to make sure a guest is taken care of (she is always offering someone something to drink), and loves to give great hugs. When she prays, she always mentions family members. If she asks God for something, when she's finished she says, "God said 'Ok'," as if she and God had a special connection. I am convinced they do.

Emma made Jesus her Lord and Savior just a few months ago. We've prayed for that since before she was ours and yet when she was ready and asking me questions, I was a little surprised. She was very practical about it, too. She just asked what she needed to do to make him her Savior. I kind of hem-hawed around thinking that I didn't want to pressure her. Finally, she just said, "Mom, what do I do? I want to belong to Him NOW!" I (laughing and crying on the inside) realized quickly that she was very serious. It was so wonderful. Her daddy got to baptize her, and she wasn't at all nervous or afraid. When she came out of the water she was so excited. She jumped up and down, grinning, and said, "That was so COOL!!" I pray that she never loses that thrill.

Because she was four months old when she came to live in our home, we missed out on those middle-of-the-night feedings. We thought of those times as "missed opportunities" to really get to know her, to bond, to memorize everything about her. Several months later, when she started awakening in the middle of the night in pain with teething, we found ourselves rushing down the hall to her room to hold her, comfort her, and get in on what we had missed in the first four months of her life.

There is so much more to our daughter's story I have not included or simply do not know. What I do know is God has a very special plan for this precious child, and He is allowing us to be witnesses to His working. Our prayer is that she will love the Lord with her life.

Maryemma has a baby brother now who we gave a biblical name, Caleb, meaning "fearless and impetuous." She loves to introduce him to everyone we meet. Sometimes when he is crying, she is the only one who can make him happy and she starts by singing Jesus Loves Me to him. I am sure that they mutually adore one another.

Caleb's Story

"He, the Lord, will cover you with His feathers, and under His wings you will find refuge. His faithfulness will be your shield and your rampart." Psalm 91:4.

At the beginning of this part of the story, my husband was still happily pastoring. I was a stay-at-home mother of five-year-old, Maryemma, and working as a freelance wedding photographer. My husband has finished his Master of Divinity degree from seminary.

He and I had always wanted a home full of children. Once again, *our* "plan" was to have our children eighteen months apart in age. So when we celebrated our daughter, Maryemma's, third birthday, I realized God surely was laughing at my "planning out" my life. He has always been, and will always be, in total control. For that I am grateful, because my plans can be shortsighted compared to His.

Shortly before Maryemma turned three, our agency workers contacted us about possibly adopting a precious little baby boy named Benjamin. He was diagnosed with a potentially fatal illness. In spite of our desire to fill our home with children, after much prayer on our part and others, every word from God seemed to be "no" or "wait." Of course, the enemy would try to tell us that by our saying "no," we were giving up all opportunity to ever adopt a second child, period. However, God's answer was loud and clear enough that we knew decisions against His will would have consequences we did not want to walk through. So, once again we prayed and praised God. It was definitely a time to give it all to God. His plan is always perfect and always on time.

We did indeed say "no" and began to pray for baby Ben's new family and for a healthy life for him. Shortly after this, Ben was placed in a family with a mother who is a nurse.

Our prayers for our family to increase continued. In June of 2006, we received another call from the staff at Loving Alternative. A birth mother in the Houston area had chosen our life book. She was a well-adjusted single mother of four other children. She knew she could not give another baby the life he needed, in her current situation. After she had delivered her son, she asked her doctor about adoption. He referred her to Loving Alternatives Adoption Agency. The director met with her and had her look through several books of families. We praised God she felt led to choose us. Her son, Austin, was brought to our area and placed in one of Loving's fantastic foster families. The agency's workers called us. After much prayer and, again, more praising, we knew this baby boy was to be ours. He was the reason God had impressed the word "wait" upon our hearts earlier. .

We were a little under-prepared for a new baby, but again, God provided in amazingly unique ways. Friends and family filled our home with little boy clothes and supplies. We were overwhelmed.

God was working His holy handiwork again with our family. On July 13, 2006, we became the proud parents to Caleb Austin, twenty-five days old, eleven pounds, twenty-two inches long. We named him Caleb because it means "fearless and impetuous." God never *has* to prove his faithfulness to us, but He does, over and over, just because He can. We are so grateful to Him.

Our family was thrilled. Caleb's big sister was sweet and gentle and loved Caleb immediately. We did get to meet his birth mother after he had been placed with us. What we expected to be an awkward visit turned out to be a sweet time of sharing. She is a very special woman.

Caleb is now a busy four-year-old boy who loves to roll around on the floor with his big sister, chase daddy around the house, and give big grunting hugs and huge slobbery kisses. We love it. Sometimes his sister doesn't love it as much. He takes his job of the 'little brother bent on pestering his big sister" very seriously. Caleb has filled our home with little boy dirt, squeals, growls, and joy. He is smart, alert, inquisitive, and stubborn. We love every part of him. Our prayer for him is that he will become a man who loves God and has a tremendous compassion for people. We praise God for our children and their stories.

ADOPTION MIRACLES ROSS AND STACI

"The true children of God are those who let God's Spirit lead them." Romans 8:14

"Many. oh Lord my God, are the wonders you have done. The things you planned for us no one can recount to you; were I to speak and tell of them, they would be too many to declare." Psalm 40:5

Miraculous things happen every day. Sometimes they are big and noticed by many. Sometimes they are just as big but known by few. I believe our journey to adoption and through adoption is long and full of every emotion possible. I guess it's best to start at the beginning.

We have been married for nine years. I think God put the idea of adoption in each of our hearts early in our lives. We can't exactly remember when, but for both of us it seems we had always been aware of, and in pursuit of, adoption. So when God brought us together, adoption was naturally something we talked about, hoped for, and planned to do someday.

After one year of marriage, the Lord led us to give Him complete control of my womb. In other words, use absolutely no form of birth control. We weren't necessarily ready to be parents, but we did it as an act of faith. During this time, we experienced so much peace and freedom in trusting God with the timing of our family.

After about a year of no birth control, one day I thought, "Weird.... I figured I would be pregnant by now." At this point, we had been married for two years and traveled quite extensively with my husband's ministry. So I wasn't "trying" to get pregnant, but I knew most people would have gotten pregnant by now.

The fact that I wasn't pregnant didn't really alarm me because, early on, I had learned to trust God completely with my womb. But after two years, then three, I began to realize, "If God had wanted me to be pregnant by now, I would be." Over the course of those years, it began to dawn on me why we weren't getting pregnant. God was calling us to adopt. This realization was hard to explain, but we knew God sometimes caused things to happen (or *not* to happen) because of what He was trying to do in us and through us. We did not see this as a disappointment because we had had a desire to adopt for so long. As crazy as this might sound, I even saw our "not getting pregnant" as God's provision so we would obey Him and adopt. I knew the adoption process would be time-consuming and expensive, and I could see how it would have been easy to abandon it, especially if we had gotten pregnant and became busy with children.

We then began to pray about and research adoption in its many forms. We weren't sure where to start or which direction this would take us. The options seemed endless and there were days I felt overwhelmed by all the agencies and options available. We finally decided to pursue a domestic adoption of a non-white child. We had always been comfortable with and felt called to have a family that looked "however God wanted it to look." We were excited to pursue what was called, in the world of adoption, a "domestic trans-racial adoption." At many agencies, non-white children were considered "hard-to-place."

I guess one of the early miracles was we even *found* our adoption agency. It was a small, Christian agency and didn't exactly come up in the "TOP 10" when we googled "adoption." Some dear friends of ours knew a family who had adopted from there and loved the agency. From their recommendation, we added it to the short list of agencies we wanted to investigate.

Because of my husband's traveling and the fact that the agency only held one orientation a year, we weren't surprised to discover he was booked the weekend of the orientation. Thankfully, and miraculously, they allowed me to attend alone. I videotaped the whole two-day orientation for my husband. This was an emotionally hard event to attend alone. I felt a little overwhelmed and sad that my husband wasn't there to experience it with me. What overshadowed those feelings, though, was the incredible sense of peace and connection I felt with the people who ran the agency. I was so touched and blown away by everything I saw and heard that weekend. The testimonies I heard and the sense of calling I saw from the agency staff really set them apart from other agencies we had visited. I was blessed to learn that the agency was a missions organization. I heard testimony from a precious birth mother. I gained a deeper understanding of the sacrifice and deep love of a birth mother for her child. Although I was there alone,

I came away from that weekend certain God was going to give us our child through this agency.

We began to work on all our paperwork, the home study, and the scrapbook. We turned everything in at the beginning of September, 2003, "pregnant" in our hearts and unsure of what to expect. I was nervous to turn everything in for many reasons. One of those reasons was that we had extensive traveling plans for the month of September, including a trip to St. Lucia for our five year wedding anniversary. I was so afraid they would call while we were gone, yet I felt certain we were supposed to turn everything in before we left.

On October twentieth, we received a call from the agency. It was only six weeks after we had turned in our paperwork. They told us a birth mother had given birth to a boy in late September, and she was pursuing adoption. She actually called the agency from the hospital after having had the baby and asked for their help. They took the baby to one of their foster families. He stayed with them while she tried to make a decision. She visited the agency to look at the profiles of waiting families and that is where the miracle took place. The caseworker gave her some books to look at, but our book was not in that group. The caseworker was actually saving our book for another birth mother whom she thought would like our family. After the birth mom left, the caseworker felt the prompting of the Holy Spirit to give our book to this young birth mother. She obeyed and called her back. This birth mother chose our family almost immediately. She was incredibly drawn to us. The miracle of this cannot be overstated.

To place a child for adoption is a selfless, painful process. To choose another family to love and to raise your child must be extremely difficult. Although I am not a birth mother who has placed her child for adoption, I can imagine the difficulty from my own experience of choosing the family who would raise our children should something happen to us. Even in doing this, we were choosing from families we knew and loved and shared life with, not strangers. To choose from a book the family who will adopt your child from a book must be so difficult. I believe it's a miracle every time a family is chosen because the Lord must reach up out of that book and speak to the heart of the birth mother, drawing her to that family. I know this miracle happens because it has happened to us twice now. It has happened to countless other families, the frequency of it doesn't diminish the incredible power of it.

After she chose us, the agency set up a meeting between the birth mother and us. We were all very nervous. We met and had an instant connection with her. She poured out her heart to us that day, sharing why she wanted to place her baby boy for adoption and why she chose us. She admired our family and our marriage and wanted her child to be raised by a mother *and* a father. She was a single mother at the time with a five-year-old daughter. She shared the difficulty of being a single mom and how she knew she could not give this baby what she wanted him to have. She desired a Christian dad and a stay-at-home mom for him. She found that in us. It was obvious to me how much she loved her baby boy and how hard this was for her to do. She knew exactly what she was sacrificing. She chose this for her child out of love. We were thrilled beyond words not only to be chosen and to have a baby on the way, but also to be given the opportunity to join in a relationship with this birth mother and her family. We were knitted together forever in our love for this precious child, and were blessed to have this mother in our lives as well.

Another miracle that took place during all this was the influence music would have in this adoption. The birth mother is very musical. She especially loves to sing. A big reason she was drawn to us was this love for music. (My husband is a musician, worship leader, and songwriter. I sing with him. Music is not just our job. It is a huge part of our lives.) She wanted her child to have music in his life from an early age. She knew he would have that with us. To skip ahead a few years, I have to say he has an incredible gift of playing the drums. He actually got his first little drum set at 15 months of age. He plays the drums daily, sometimes for two hours. At the risk of sounding like an overly proud parent, I'll just say he is very gifted with a great deal of natural talent. What a miracle that he was placed into our family where that talent could be easily discovered and nurtured so early in his life. It's not common for kids to be exposed to music at the level our son was so early in his life. He is already using this gift to glorify God.

One week after our meeting with the birthmother, the adoption took place. Everything happened so fast. The placement ceremony was very special and emotional. The birth mother spent some time with the baby that day before we came to the agency. Once we arrived, we spent a couple of hours together, talking and sharing stories. She brought many gifts to send with us. Saying "good-bye" was the hardest part. She said a precious prayer over her little boy and blessed him. After she left, we did all the paperwork and met with the foster family to gather his things and get last-minute instructions. Since he was our first child, we were a bit overwhelmed, and the baby started crying toward the end. He cried almost the whole three hours home. We had never been so happy to see our house. A friend had left gifts and balloons to welcome us home.

Even before we turned in our paperwork, I felt a certainty and peace that God was going to give us a son. I had prayed to God asking for a son for many years, and when he blessed us with this adoption, I knew that I wanted our baby to have the Biblical name, Samuel. It means "God has heard." For his middle name, we kept one of the names his birthmother gave him, Isaac, meaning "laughter."

The first six weeks with our new little boy were difficult. I was learning how to be a mom for the first time without the benefit of nine months of pregnancy to plan and to prepare emotionally. He was trying to adjust and to bond with us after being with his birth mother for nine months and with his foster mother for six weeks. Both he and I cried a lot! I sang to him, and we both adjusted to the newness in our lives. He learned to trust me with his needs, and I learned to trust God with mine. It was a time of stretching and growing for each of us. I was glad when those first six weeks were over and our bonding was much more secure. He seemed to change almost overnight around Christmas time. Until then, he had been struggling. He had cried and seemed fretful much of the time. At Christmas, he suddenly became relaxed and happy, the secure little boy he has been ever since.

Early on in this adoption process I had prayed God would give us a flexible baby. For the first five years of our marriage, I had traveled with my husband most of the time. Routinely, we would be on the road about fifteen days a month. I wanted to continue traveling with him once we adopted a baby, so I prayed God would give us an easy-going child who would adapt to the ever-changing schedules of being on the road. God did that and more.

Our son was such an attraction. He was easily trained to become a part of our ministry to others. He smiled a lot, loved the music, and was happy to be by my side all the time. He is a very affectionate child and never minded sitting in my lap for hours whether on planes or sitting through long worship services. He likes music so much. He is happy to watch the band rehearse and watch the whole music scene. When most kids would become bored or restless, he would happily stay and watch. He loved summer camp, and always had such deep relationships with the guys in our band. Having him with us on the road for the first three years of his life was such a blessing -- for him, for us, and for others. Everywhere we went, we were able to share about the miracle of adoption. So many people were made aware of adoption in ways they hadn't been before. His sweet spirit is a draw for people. He has a way of making people feel special. It is a gift God uses to draw people to Himself. What a blessing that it started at such an early age.

When our little boy was almost two years old, we decided to pursue another adoption. It was hard to know the right time to turn in the picture album and paperwork. If I based it on our own experience, I would expect a baby in three months. However, I knew things could take longer. We felt ready in September 2005. I turned everything in. We began to wait. It turned out God had a very different experience in mind for us the second time around. Rather than getting a call three months later, we received *the* call one year later. I was happy being a mom, but it was arduous to wait this long and not have any idea when God would bring us another child. We were still busy with our ministry and church, but I felt ready for a little brother or sister for our son.

During the three years between our two sons, two "carrots" were dangled in front of us. The agency would tell us about a situation and allow us to pray. The idea was to be sure God was saying the same thing to both sides of this adoption. Maybe the toughest, most painful call we had to make was to tell the agency the child who was ready for adoption was not to be ours. As much as we had prayed for a child, we felt God was saying this child was not ours. I was fearful we would hurt the birth mother, miss God's best for our family, or generally mess things up somehow. As it turned out, that child belonged to another adoptive family perfectly suited for him.

The second "almost" adoption was from a sister agency which had a child ready for adoption. We met the birth mom and seemed to connect. The birth father was serving in the military overseas. It would take at least fourteen days to get a signed waiver of interest from him. In the meantime, the birth mom decided to parent temporarily. After two weeks on the emotional roller coaster of this birth mom's indecision, we were emotionally exhausted. She decided to parent. We were actually relieved, even though we were deeply disappointed. We knew if God had closed the door on that adoption, He must have another plan for us. He knew exactly which child He was preparing for us.

After two months of grieving over this failed adoption, God opened the door again. Our agency called and told us a birth mother had chosen our book. Could we come in and meet the birth-grandmother as soon as possible? Of course we could! After the year we had just experienced, we were ready and excited. We went into this adoption with a sense of anticipation and peace. This birth mother was pregnant with her second child, a boy.

One of the miracles I noticed during this time was how similar the situation was to our first adoption. Both of the babies were bi-racial (a white birth mother and black birth father.) Both birth mothers were already single moms of daughters and were aware of the realities of parenting. Both knew they wanted their sons to have a Christian father and mother and with a certainty were ready to place their child for adoption with us.

We spent a wonderful morning visiting with the birth grandmother. At this point the birth mother, eight and a half months pregnant, and age eighteen was not sure she was ready to meet us. We were disappointed not to get to meet her and begin a relationship with her. Her mother was wonderful, and she shared all about her daughter and granddaughter. She told us her daughter had struggled, knowing she could not give this child the kind of life she wanted him to have.

She was still in relationship with the birth father. Neither of them felt they could parent this child as he deserved. Both the birth mother and the birth father agreed adoption was the right decision. One of the miracles during this time was the influence our first son had in this process. The birth parents were excited about their little boy growing up in a family with an older brother. That was special to me also because I desired for our first son to have a little buddy. God provided for that hope of mine.

We left the meeting with the birth grandmother having peace and knowing that all we could do now was wait for the baby to be born. He arrived in late October 2006, two months later.

He was born on his due date, and we picked him up two days later. This was a new experience for us – adopting a two-day old baby straight from the hospital. Our first son was six weeks old at his placement. We were nervous, even though this was our second time, it was new in many ways. It was at the hospital. We had not yet met the birth mother and still weren't sure if we would. We didn't know what to expect in terms of the family's feelings. Were they still sure about this? Were they going to change their minds? And of course, what would our new baby be like?

When we arrived, the agency staff met us and took us to the room where the placement would occur. At that point, the birth mother was in the process of signing the papers to relinquish her parental rights. This was a heart-wrenching time for her. Most birth mothers have to make this choice twice: before the baby is born, when they choose a family, and again after the bay is born. It's much harder the second time. They have been through hours of labor and here is this tiny baby to whom they are saying good-bye. The birth mother's body still bears the scars of childbirth, but there is no child to help ease the pain. There's no immediate reward. Just empty arms and pain. I have cried at both of our placements, and for many months afterward, thinking about and praying for our birth mothers. How hard it must have been to do what they did! How difficult not to have a baby to feed or hold after nine months of carrying this precious child so near their hearts.

So sitting there in that hospital, knowing she was just a few doors down the hall making one of the hardest decisions of her life, was incredibly emotional for us. It was weird to hope that she would go through with the decision, knowing the pain it would cause her and her family--but also knowing if she didn't go through with it, there would be pain and heartbreak for us and our family.

Adoption is very messy. It is beautiful and full of God, but it's not simple or tidy. There is much to sort through and many miracles to watch unfold every time an adoption takes place. It's such a beautiful picture of the way God has adopted each of us. Our adoption as sons and daughters into God's family is messy, too. It involves repentance and brokenness and usually some tears. But in the end, this gift of life God has provided through Jesus, this way back to Him after things were messed up by sin, brings a perfect reconciliation of our brokenness and His holiness. Similarly, adoption is a wonderful reconciliation of physical brokenness -- husband and wife are broken because they can't conceive, and a child is born without a whole family. It all comes together to create a new, whole, un-broken family. Two broken things are made whole, for the glory of God.

After a while, our caseworker came back from meeting with the birth mother, holding our new baby boy. We were overjoyed! She had made her decision, and we were adding a son to our family. Praise God! We held him and looked at him and took lots of pictures. Our first son was mesmerized by him and was so sweet and tender with his new baby brother. It was a wonderful, joyous time.

After being with the baby for about an hour, it became clear to us that his birth mother was still not ready to meet with us. We were disappointed because we had really wanted to have the opportunity to get to know her -- to hug her, to thank her, and to love her. We still hope and pray we'll get that chance one day. Her mother did come to meet with us and to say good-bye to her grandson. Her husband was with her, whom we met for the first time. They both cried over Jude. Then we all stood in a circle and prayed. We prayed for this precious new life and for our family. We prayed for the birth family and for all the lives this little boy had already touched and would touch in the future. God moved among us, and after we prayed, we took more pictures and said our final good-byes.

We started our three-hour drive home. It was much more relaxed than that first drive home. We stopped at Wal-Mart to get him some sleepers as I had forgotten to bring him some clothes. We even stopped and had dinner at a restaurant with our 2-day old baby. Once we were home, we decided to give him the Biblical name Jude which means "praise and thanks."

At the time of this writing, our sons are five and two. Time goes by so fast, as most parents know. It feels like I blinked and we were bringing our first baby home. I blinked again and I have two little boys. We are so happy God has blessed us by building our family through adoption. We know that not everyone gets to experience the blessing of adoption and to see the fruit it bears in all the lives it touches. We know some arrive at adoption after a painful process of infertility, and others come to it with open arms. In the end though, I think those who are touched by adoption will agree it is a miraculous and blessed gift. It changes us and opens our eyes. It leaves us forever imprinted with the image of God and the whisper of His love in our lives.

Our God is the God of miracles. We are so blessed to have been adopted into His eternal victorious family.

DREAMS COME TRUE

As we were thinking it was nearing the time for us to add another child to our ever-growing family, I looked back to how our two sons came to us. Neither was a carbon copy of the other. Yet, we could see God was definitely involved in each of those stories. Maybe we should choose a different agency, one closer to our home. In the quandary, we had put decisions on hold. I could not dismiss the idea that it was time to seek another child. Yet, I was deeply unsettled for several months. Somewhere during this time in the midst of all my indecision in early August, I had a dream. The dream went something like this:

I was called by the caseworkers of Loving Alternative to come in for a "meeting." Immediately after we arrived for this "meeting", I was handed a baby and told, "Here's your new baby!" In my surprise (as I had absolutely no idea we were coming to adopt a new baby), I looked down and saw that our new baby was a black baby girl. However, a few minutes later, a woman came to me and said, "We've made a mistake…this is actually your new baby." She handed me a white baby girl. {In my dream I thought nothing of this.} Soon after that I was led to a hospital room to meet the birth mother. On the bed was a woman who looked to be about 40 years old. She was a white woman with shoulder length brownish-blonde hair. She had people standing around her, some black and some white. I looked at her and we just stared at each other for a while. Then I burst into tears and ran from the room. I spent the rest of my dream away from everyone crying and crying for this woman. When my mom asked why I was crying, I said, "I just can't stop hurting for her." I knew she was hurting deeply and that she had gone through something very hard. I awakened from the dream without more details.

That was the end of the dream. At the time, I thought the dream was strange and mostly "just a dream." I didn't put much stock in it. I did go so far as to tell my husband and a friend about it, but beyond that, I didn't necessarily see it as prophetic or connected to our upcoming adoption.

After our busy summer with youth and family camps, I saw that Doris from Loving Alternative had left me a message. On her message, she said, with an urgency in her voice, that she needed me to call her back immediately. She had something important to share with me. Two distinct thoughts ran through my head after hearing the message. Was something going on with Sam or Jude's birthmothers? Or did Doris have a new birth mother who she wanted us to meet? I was excited and hopeful as I called her back immediately.

She told me that she was calling about a new birthmother. Doris had been meeting with a woman who was about to start the process of choosing a family. Her name was Christi, a young woman who had been living in a dark time of her life. She was raised in a Christian home, but as an adult made choices that had serious consequences. She had been addicted to drugs for most of her adult life. This pregnancy was the result of being raped by three men at a party where people were doing drugs. She found she was pregnant approximately four months into it. She didn't know where to turn. Because of her drug addiction and other destructive choices, she was estranged from most of her family including her parents. Desperate, she called her brother, the one family member with whom she still had a relationship. He had a contact who could help her. Soon Christi ended up in Fatherheart Maternity Home. She had been drug-free since she was made aware of the pregnancy and had been working with counselors to deal with her trauma and grief. After several months, she had made the decision to pursue adoption for her baby.

Doris called to see if I could get a book together as quickly as possible and send it to her. In my excitement and joy over this opportunity, I said I would do everything possible to get it to her within a week. During this phone call, I learned that Christi was going to have a girl, but that she did not know what the race her baby would be. Therefore, the agency had a limited pool of family life books to show her. Doris had felt led to contact us because she knew we would be open to any race. In any case, it was the Lord's work to connect us with Christi.

Once I hung up and began to reflect on our conversation, it all hit me. I remembered the dream and realized that it was, in fact, prophetic. God had given me that dream to prepare me for this relationship with Christi and this new baby.

Everything about the dream was playing itself out in reality. In the dream we were given a black baby girl, then a white baby girl, thus the ambiguity on the race. In reality the baby was a girl, but the race was unknown. In the dream I looked at Christi and hurt for her without knowing the reason for my pain. My compassion for her was a God given spiritual connection. Christi was traumatized having been raped by three men.

Doris had not previously heard the story of the dream. She just somehow *knew* that we needed to get a book in for Christi to look at when choosing a family for her baby. When the story of the dream became known, Doris said that she would have been surprised if Christi had not chosen us. By then we agreed.

Psalm 139 says that we were knit together in our mother's womb. We are "fearfully and wonderfully" made. There may be a horrendous situation surrounding a child's conception. Even David was told that he was conceived in his mother's sin. But whatever the situation, like Joseph was able to tell his brothers, "You meant this for evil, but God meant it for good." This baby girl's beginning was not the way God would have chosen. But, He obviously is using it for good as He chose her for our family. And it is so very good!

Naomi is beautiful with her flashing dark eyes and olive complexion. Fun and feisty describe her. Sweet but tough are traits she has learned from playing with Sam and Jude during their rough games and loud yelling. Beyond "social" describes her as she waves, smiles, flirts, and says hi to just about everyone.

More than a year after placement, here are some notes to Christi: "You are so important and special to us. I hope that you will never forget that we value you and desire a relationship with you. At placement we gave you the charm bracelet with the cross, symbolizing your sacrifice of love for your daughter. This year's charm is a charm called, "A Mother's Love." You showed a true picture of a mother's love to little Rachel (Naomi) when you gave her up to God and allowed her to be placed into our family. The only way I will ever understand how you followed through with the placement decision is you had God's help, strength, and courage. You have shown me what true sacrificial love looks like. I hope that every time you look at the charms, you will be reminded of the way you showed her the greatest love possible. Naomi will always know how much you loved her then and still love her. You, her first mother showed her true sacrificial love. Her placement into our family was done in love. I pray that if you ever have doubts or come upon hard times, you will look at this bracelet and remember there is a family who truly loves you and prays for you. We believe that God has a great plan for your life and this is only the beginning for you."

Ross said, "People were always telling me how different it would be to have a girl, especially after having two boys. I assumed they were right, but I really had no idea. It's difficult to explain what it has done to my heart to have this little lady invade our home and invade my heart. Her smile always makes me smile, and her tears have more influence over me than they should. It's not just an expression when I say, 'God help me if my daughter ever learns the kind of power she has over me!' I am completely undone by my little princess, and I am so very thankful that the Lord has given her to us. What an honor! What a responsibility! What a joy!"

Ross has found a whole different responsibility emerging with the addition of a sweet daughter to raise, love, and protect. He is enjoying the feminine addition to the family with lace, pink ribbons and frilly clothing. Both Ross and I have found the gift of nurturing this delightful little girl a new adventure. We are surprised to learn how different it is than it was in the early years with the rough and tumble boys. We are so blessed by her every day. Her sweet countenance and joy just light up our home. She is the perfect fit for us and we are so thankful for her.

AN UNFINISHED STORY

Words elicit feelings. Words elicit memories. What feelings or memories does the word adoption bring to your mind? For some it is love, acceptance, or hope. For others it is irresponsibility, abandonment, or rejection.

This was a private adoption. No agency was involved. A nineteen-year-old unwed pregnant girl had come to our town to escape the shame her pregnancy would have caused her parents had she stayed at home. She'd had one year of college. Her parents merely told her they would not "finance her 'misadventure.'" Were they thinking of the cost of an abortion? I don't know. This was prior to Roe vs. Wade. All we knew about her is stated above.

My husband and I had a six and a half year old daughter and had been trying for over a year to conceive another. My doctor tested both my husband and me and found no reason not to get pregnant. He then suggested adoption with these words. "I have a girl who is pregnant. She comes from good, European stock. Her baby would fit nicely into your family." We could talk it over and let him know in a week or 10 days.

Because we'd had one child, the doctor surmised that adopting a baby would help us to relax about trying so hard to conceive and then perhaps we would.

Back then our motives weren't exactly pure and thoughtful. We still wanted a biological baby boy to "carry on the name," so maybe the doctor's idea of adoption would, in deed, do the trick.

We adopted Jeff. He was 2 days old. He was the most beautiful, lovable, bright eyed, alert, perfect baby we'd ever seen. Even then, I knew God gives adopted children something special. Not until 33 years later did I give another thought to his birth mom.

Jeff did fit right into our family. And the doctor was right. I did conceive and delivered that longed-for namesake one year and three weeks after Jeff's birth.

All these years Jeff has known nothing about his actual heritage accept the little we'd known from the doctor. He has no medical, social, or physical records. He doesn't know from whom he gets his stature or his intense interest in classical music or his ability to work with his hands. He doesn't know who blessed him with his compassionate spirit or his ability to draw children to himself. He has felt some missing pieces.

Yes, he had the love and nurture of two parents and a sister and brother who treated him as a "real" sibling. But today it would have been different.

Thirteen years ago God called me to a ministry to young women who find themselves in an unplanned pregnancy. God has given me an intense passion for adoption--the way this ministry does it.

Almost immediately after coming here and reading files to get an idea of how things are done, I had my *first* thought of Jeff's birth mother. I began to pray for her, a thing I had never thought to do before. Next the thought came to me that probably she had had no counseling and might not have worked through the pain of grief, the sadness, loneliness, emptiness, shame, blame, and even secrecy. Maybe if I found her, I could help her as I was attempting to help the young women who came my way here in the ministry.

I often talked to God about her and even gave him some ideas about how He could introduce us to one another. Over the years, nothing solid happened for us to meet. Eventually I found an organization in the state where Jeff had been born that had licensed workers eligible to locate whichever leg of the adoption triangle one wanted to find. I pursued that route. My motive was to find information that I could share with Jeff that would answer some questions for him. Where did he get his size and his strong athletic abilities? Where did he get his love for classical music— never having heard it in our home? Even his size and shape as an adult did not line up with the rest of us.

After almost two years, the woman doing the searching called me. She said, "You are not going to meet her." I asked what happened.

She said, "I got her on the phone and introduced myself. I told her that I wanted to talk to her about a time she lived in Tucson, Arizona."

The woman screamed into the phone, "*I never lived in Tucson, Arizona!*"

My lady said, "If you recall, it was forty years ago."

The woman replied with another scream, "*This is inappropriate!*" and hung up.

I assured my lady that she did all she could do and we would just have to leave the rest up to God.

My thoughts were consumed with her report through the rest of that day and into the next. When I prayed to God about it, I felt that He said,

"You *thought* I wanted *you* to find her so *you* could help her. No. I wanted *you* to find her so *I* could help her."

What a revelation! Now when I pray for her and her family, I always thank God that He is helping her as well as the rest of her family. I know that God often gets our attention when we least expect it, and when we are at the lowest point of our lives. I cannot imagine what it would be like to have kept a "deep dark secret" for forty years and have someone find it out. But nothing is too difficult for God. I can do nothing for this birth mom. But that is okay. God is helping her.

HAROLD AND CECEILA

Sadly, negative stories about adoption are the only ones that make it into the media because they are the "sensational" stories, but they can give adoption a bad reputation.

Harold and Cecelia adopted two children. They are great kids who "function" remarkably well with good self-images and strong security about who they are. On the other hand, their grandmother lived in daily fear that someone would "come and take back" one of those two special children who had grown up as the legal children of her daughter and son-in-law.

After fifteen years, "Gramma" went to an annual banquet sponsored by the adoption agency that placed her grandchildren with her daughter's family. She "table hopped" talking to as many of the adoptive families as possible. Then, there was a speaker who was an adoptive parent. Her eyes were opened, and she was set free!

On the way home with Harold and Cecelia, Gramma finally shared her "secret fear." She had lived with this fear for fifteen years, but with all the conversations with other adoptive families, and then hearing the testimony of the speaker as an adoptive parent, she had finally been set free from that fear.

"You shall know the truth, and the truth will set you free."

SOME CALL THEM COINCIDENCES.
WE CALL THEM MIRACLES.

"For the LORD God is a sun and shield;
The LORD will give grace and glory;
No good thing will He withhold
From those who walk uprightly.
O LORD of hosts, Blessed is the man who trusts in You!"
Psalm 84:11-12

During our first four years of marriage and no miraculous pregnancy and baby, I continued to struggle with myself, with the Lord, with rejoicing over my friends' pregnancies and babies, and to mourn over my own seeming barrenness. Perhaps adoption was the route we needed to take. Because we served as missionaries in Ireland, we attended an adoption orientation in the social services sector in Ireland. We were told we could expect a home study between five and ten years in the future. The list was that long. Even though my husband is British, we couldn't adopt in England because we weren't resident there. Our only option was an adoption from the United States. Every year we come home to Texas to fundraise, furlough, and visit family. In 2004, we applied to three different agencies, besides the small Christian one near our home. We wanted to increase our chances of having a baby soon. Then we went back to life in Ireland.

Here, I'll take you back four years. We married in 1999 at ages twenty-seven and thirty-one with gratitude and joy to God for leading us together. I assumed that children would come soon. I have always loved and wanted children, and I felt that part of God's calling on my life was to be a mother. I did get pregnant soon and was so excited I told everyone as soon as I found out. I never expected to lose the baby at three months gestation. We were devastated! Our comfort was the thought that we would get pregnant again. We didn't.

My husband graduated from seminary in the spring of 2000, and we were in Ireland that autumn. It was very interesting and different from what I had expected. In the back of my mind, I was still hoping to get pregnant. I found a place to serve with the children at church, and I became known as the organizer of big projects or events for evangelism. These were good distractions from the emotional pressure mounting in my heart, and our marriage, from not yet having children.

As usual each year, we returned to Texas still waiting and praying. We stayed busy. My in-laws from England came to Texas for a long visit during February. The last Friday in February, we were on our way to Houston to show them around NASA. As was our custom, we would preach at as many churches as possible during our furlough. The plan during this trip was to preach at a church in the Houston area during our trip to sightsee. While on that drive, we got a call on our cell phone from our adoption caseworker. She said a birth mom had chosen us. She gave us the details of the situation—a healthy birth mom, a healthy pregnancy and a healthy baby. She said she would give us time to pray about it. We told her we didn't need any time to pray. We had been praying for this for years.

The biggest miracle of our adoption was the way every detail fell into place from that point on. It was as if it had been planned out for us ahead of time. The birth mom wanted to meet us on the following Wednesday. That day, her parents and sisters would be available before they went on vacation. Interestingly, the baby was due on Ireland's holiday, St. Patrick's Day.

Our meeting with her and her family was quite overwhelming for us. We met with her, her parents, and her two adult sisters. They were very nice. It was awkward for us because they felt they knew us quite well from our scrapbook. We hadn't even known they existed a week before. I was worried I would say something to change their minds, but they were still sure of us even after meeting us. Maybe that was a miracle too.

I was keenly aware from a previous experience that this birth mom could change her mind at any time during the process. I kept as busy as possible for those few weeks, and I didn't buy anything. I was afraid that making purchases would cause me to begin to imagine how things could be. If she changed her mind and my heart was all wrapped up in the dream, that would give a whole new meaning to the word "devastation."

On March 23, 2005, our dream came true. She delivered a healthy baby girl. We named her an Anglicized version of a Gaelic name which means "*dream.*" We gave our daughter her birth mom's middle name in her honor. On the morning before her placement with us in the afternoon, my mom and I bought all the basics we would need.

How can we name all the miracles this event and our sweet daughter's life (as well as our birth mom's life and her choice) culminated for us? First, that a birth mom would choose a family who doesn't live in the United States, was, to me, a big hurdle.

Also. we have a dog, "Lady," whom we love. Maybe Lady would "put off" any prospective birth mom. We learned later that our birth mom would only look at family scrapbooks with dogs in them. What I thought was a weakness was really a strength for us.

There was also the miracle of surprise. How refreshing to be surprised on the way to Houston when we weren't even thinking of it. The Lord Jesus had been working on things without our knowledge, even as we had trusted Him to do. The agency's worker says another miracle was that the birth mom chose us as her baby's family the day before we arrived in the United States for our annual furlough. This caused everything to work out so she and her family could meet us before she had her baby.

Another miracle was my British husband had a Social Security number. One of the legal requirements to adopt was we both needed to have a Social Security number. My husband, along with a few other students, had gotten their cards to study at a seminary in the United States. A few days after he got his, the government stopped giving out Social Security cards to foreign seminary students.

The day of our daughter's placement was a wonderful day for us. It was extremely difficult for this new young mom, as one could imagine. For me, the major miracle was that she, as far as I know and am told, didn't second-guess her decision of placing her daughter with us. It's a great relief to me that, so far, she hasn't ever regretted her decision.

Our sweet little girl is the perfect child—smart, sweet, healthy, and easy-going. Every day we are blessed with her and the miraculous ways God turned around our circumstances and made us a family of three. Now, the next big miracle on the list would be a baby brother or sister for our daughter. That is another story.

BLESSINGS CAME IN TRIPLE PORTIONS

"He blessed them, and their numbers greatly increased.."
Psalm 107:38a

"He lifted the needy out of their affliction and increased their families."
Psalm 107:41

We had always thought of our home as teeming with children. While we were in Ireland, as missionaries, we could not adopt internationally. Ashlin, our first daughter was getting older. Our vision was to have our children close in age.

When the time came for us to leave the mission field and Ireland, we did not know what God had for us next. There was a recurring sense of "children." I did not know what that meant exactly. I was working with the children in our churches in Ireland. Perhaps that would be what I would continue to do in America. Or, maybe the "children" would be ours. We were so unsure. We didn't stop praying for more children for our family. Our thinking was "one at a time" a boy or a girl. Yet, when Ashlin prayed, she always prayed for a brother *and* a sister.

When we did return to America, we couldn't start the adoption process until Tim got a job. God's hand seemed to be involved in Tim's taking a position with Child Protective Services. He began the job in April 2008, by August, he knew that sort of work was not for him. I then began to apply for full time work as a teacher. The recurring "children" theme was still foremost in our minds. If Tim's working with the children in CPS wasn't to be, then perhaps I was to go back to the classroom and become a teacher of children. No doors for that "plan" opened.

In our unsettled plans for what to do as a couple and a family, we happened on to a newspaper ad for Christian Homes and Family Services. They were seeking families to foster children. We made the decision to follow that ad and began the process of qualifying to foster. Our hearts were not to just foster. We wanted children we could legally adopt for all time.

We had prayed and waited a long time. We needed to be "pro-active." Now, we felt it was time for us to "do something" to get the process going. It was then that we made the decision to transfer to Child Protective Services in order to foster to adopt. Our hearts seemed to be more ready to risk taking children and having to let them go. With our first adoption with Ashlin, our hearts were fragile. This time we felt more secure. But we did not want to have children in our home and perhaps have to return them—more for Ashlin's sake than for our own.

By October 1, we were fully prepped and licensed as a foster family. We had agreed to foster up to three siblings under Ashlin's age. She was three at that time. I told our caseworker, in passing, that I was a "card carrying" Native American, Chickasaw Tribe. We also planned to apply with that tribe next. Giving her that knowledge was only if it would give us an advantage in working with Child Protective Services.

My dad has always had a great sense of family history. His grandmother was a Christian. She was the first person who rejoiced with him when he told her that he had become a Christian as a child in church. She was a full-blooded Chickasaw as well as a praying woman. Her mother had been a member of the Christian Indian Women's Missionary Union in her town. She had brought her daughter up to love the Lord as well. My dad's mom didn't believe in the Lord until much later than her dad had. However, he always knew that his mom prayed for him, his wife, and his children. There was a sense of purpose in their "Indian-hood" even though they were from a small, relatively unknown tribe outside of Oklahoma.

So, when the CPS caseworker called to say there were Indian heritage children who were available for adoption, our ears perked up. We prayed about it a lot and not long after, we told our caseworker to put our names forward. The oldest was six months older than Ashlin. That was not what we'd planned. It was scary. After the staff talked it over, they told us we could temporarily foster. This is the only way we could be considered for the adoption plan of these three children. I decided to set a "fleece" out before the Lord. I said, "God, if these children are Chickasaw, we will take them." They *were Chickasaw*. We had our answer.

Tim still needed a job. He had been looking for three months. He happened to walk in to a school district's employment office the day they had let go their previous bus driver. Tim got the job. They trained him immediately. Miracles were piling up.

We continued to be concerned for Ashlin should these children need to leave our home. We kept telling her that they were with us *for now*. We didn't know anything beyond that.

It was so very hard. These children were, Gigi, six months older than Ashlin; but not as secure or mature. The boys, Philip and James, were two and three years old. At first none knew how to obey parents, or follow any instructions. Ashlin had been "queen of the hill." She now had to share her things as well as the attention of her parents and grand parents. After one month Ashlin said, "My life hurts! These kids need to go home." Now, more than a year later, Ashlin has changed along as have her siblings. Ashlin is more loving, sharing, and affectionate. Gigi, Philip, and James have grown to fit into the routine of real family living.

It was during this difficult transition, that I reflected my thoughts in my journal. Here are my words: "I am amazed. I am thinking of Mary and how she must have had a hard time, even though she was in a crucial ministry—bearing and having baby Jesus amidst scorn and aloneness and in a dirty, cold manger. Surely the baby cried—all babies do. She must have had sleepless nights. Perhaps Joseph wasn't all she had hoped for. Was he doing this just out of duty? Or was he awestruck by the idea? Or did he not believe her but knew that God had spoken to him anyway. All of this is to say that I have a little time to reflect that we're sitting, standing, walking in the middle of a miracle—a definite God thing with these children. But, it is not easy! I don't love them as much as I want to and they don't love Ashlin as much as I'd like them to. There is so much to be concerned about the future if it works out for us to have them permanently. At this point, I think it will. We're headed that way."

We all went through family counseling. James got tubes in his ears. Now, I look at the children. They play well together. They listen. Actually, they came with teachable spirits. This helped. With my consistency and the security of the family we all learned to relax. Tim is good. He often says, "Don't make more work for yourself and don't let them make more work for you." I have two healthy activities for each one each day. With the reliable scheduling, they are always ready for naps in the afternoons. Even when they pass around sicknesses, they know that I am there whenever they need me.

All three were finalized in June 2009. The church had a beautiful adoption party that was videoed. Each child was given a special, personal prayer. The original foster family and our family were all a part of the celebration.

I wonder if we had known what was ahead of us on this journey at the onset, we might not have taken the risk. Looking back we see God's hand in it every step of the way. We are so glad. Otherwise we could have backed out and missed this beautiful picture He has painted of our "forever family."

GOD'S HAND WORKS THROUGH HIS TIME

"Hope deferred makes the heart sick. But a longing fulfilled is a tree of life." Proverbs 13:12

Every child born into this world is a miracle in itself, but sometimes it takes a special miracle to get a child into the arms of the parents God intended him to have. Our beautiful little blue–eyed blonde son is such a miracle.

My husband and I got married when he was twenty-five and I was thirty-three. I had just about given up hope of ever finding the love of my life, when out of the blue, there he was. Because I was already in my thirties and could hear and feel my biological clock ticking, we started trying to have a baby right away. After two or three years with no luck, we decided God needed some help. We went to a fertility clinic, but we gave that up after nine months because of the emotional toll; month after month of disappointments were more than we could bear. The financial drain was staggering as well. Looking back now, I can see so clearly that was not what God had wanted for us. The fertility drugs didn't seem to work. Today, I can honestly say I am glad I did not get pregnant. If I had, we would have missed out on the little boy who is truly a gift from God.

We had sort of talked around the idea of adoption, but I could not give up the hope of having a child biologically. While we were going to the fertility clinic, the doctors had discovered that I had fibroid tumors in my uterus. As long as they were not bothering me, there was no need to remove them. As I approached my forties, my doctor told me the tumors were growing and I really needed a hysterectomy. For almost three years, I fought having the surgery because I didn't want to accept the finality of it. For three years, I prayed and prayed God would give us a baby before my chance was gone. Six weeks before my forty-third birthday, I finally had the surgery I needed for so long. Two days before my surgery, we went to the prospective adoptive couples' orientation at a near-by maternity home connected with a small Christian adoption agency. We left there knowing with absolute certainty that if we were to adopt a baby, it would come through that organization. Isn't God's timing amazing? It was like He was opening another door for me before He completely closed the first one.

We did all the required paperwork and put together a photo album that depicted our life stories. We put it all in the mail to the agency and continued to pray. (A girl who has made the decision to place her baby for adoption looks at those albums and chooses the couple who will raise her baby.) After getting our album in, we waited almost two more years.

We were close to the point of accepting it might not have been God's plan for us to raise a child. The interesting thing was we were beginning to be okay about it. I believe our submissiveness to God's will was what He had wanted from us before He could bless us with a child. In early July 2005, on a Wednesday night, we got the call telling us we had been chosen by a young girl desiring to place her baby with us. We were ecstatic! Everything started to happen at once. We began a whirlwind of activity to complete everything required by the state standards.

We went to meet her on Friday of the next week. We liked her immediately. She seemed to be assured she had chosen the right couple. The baby was not due until early August, so we went home thinking we had three more weeks to wait. But two days later, we got the call that our little boy had been born. His birth mother had developed toxemia and had to have an emergency C-section. We were warned the next couple of days could be very tricky. She had called the birth father to come to the hospital. (That is never a good sign.) In this case, she was having thoughts that together, they could raise their baby and be a family. Her idea began to become a reality when a couple of days later, the agency told us she had decided not to place her baby for adoption.

I don't think I can adequately describe the devastation we felt. The people with whom we had been dealing at the agency were wonderfully kind and supportive. Because of their compassionate spirits, they were genuinely sorrowful for us. They said the emotions we were feeling were comparable to those of a couple who had suffered a miscarriage or even the death of their child. We didn't understand why it had happened, but neither of us blamed God or railed against Him. Even in our grief, we knew there was a reason for what had happened.

We went on with our lives, outwardly, as if nothing had ever happened. Inside, we were grieving the loss of our dream. We both wondered what was happening to our little baby boy. Was he being taken care of? Was he happy and content? For almost four months, we heard nothing. Then, in early November, we got another call from the agency telling us the birth mother and father had both signed the relinquishment papers. They wanted us to have the baby...if we still wanted him. If we still wanted him? Of course we wanted him! In our hearts, he had been ours from the moment of his birth. Three days later, we walked through the door of the agency office. Our baby's birth mother hugged me and then placed him in my arms.

He is four now. We managed to get through the "terrific twos" and and the "theatrical threes". He is an absolute joy and so much fun. He is beautiful, bright and sweet natured. We still marvel at how blessed we are to have such a wonderful child. We know beyond the shadow of a doubt that he is the child God meant for us to have all along. We still don't understand why it took almost four months after his birth for it to happen, but we know that was part of God's plan, too. Maybe it was for his birth mother's benefit. She is as precious to God as we are. Maybe He wanted her to try to parent so she could see that raising him by herself was not the right thing for her, or for him. Whatever the reason, we don't dwell on the time we didn't have with him. We just cherish our times with him now.

I know we don't love our child any more than biological parents love their natural children, but I do believe adoptive parents might be more attuned to the fact that their children truly are gifts from God. After years of pain from empty arms--and the heartache and disappointments that go along with that, finally holding a child in our arms and knowing we are a family seems like a long-awaited miracle has come true.

FATHER'S DAY

"How great is the love the Father has lavished on us, that we should be called children of God!" I John 3:1

Today is Father's Day--a day that means more to me than I can say. Many of our friends know I have two adopted daughters. Father's Day is especially meaningful to me because of that. What some do not know is that my own father doesn't believe in God. I wasn't raised in a Christian home. However, like my daughters, I feel I have been adopted--adopted into the kingdom of faith.

Fathers have such a profound influence on their children. How does a son come to have faith when all he hears growing up is religion and the Word of God put down? Is it because of my father's sister and her husband, my Aunt Joan and Uncle Bob, prayed for me for years? They then rejoiced with me when I was saved and baptized. Is it because of a powerful, spiritual, and beautiful wife who loved and nurtured me for years before I truly accepted the Lord? Or is it because of a small but awesome congregation that serves children, youth, and families?

I don't remember the exact moment when I came to believe. But I do have a good feeling inside when I think about those people who prayed for me, and when I live by faith. Sometimes it's hard with my background and upbringing to live by faith. It is a faith that knows God, our Father, will be here providing for me and blessing my family and me.

Yes, fathers have a profound influence on their children. Through my experiences and the faith in God that has been growing within me, I have come to believe that God's design for family includes a godly father. A godly father fulfills his responsibilities to provide, protect, and guide his family.

Another reason Father's Day is special to me is that two different birth mothers have agreed with this design. They have entrusted me with their baby girls. They had faith I would guide these children in this design.

There was a time when I thought I wouldn't be a father. After ten years and several attempts at invitro-fertilization, we finally conceived twins, a boy we named Nolan and a girl we named Sierra. Complications developed at twenty-two weeks. The babies were born premature and did not survive.

I remember people trying to help us in our grief by telling us it just wasn't a part of God's plan. I don't believe it was in God's plan to take our babies. I don't want to believe in a God who would take our babies. It is our faith in God's love and God's grace that got us through the grief.

Since it seemed we were not able to have children, we began to pray for God to remove the desire for children from our hearts. God answered our prayers. But it wasn't this particular prayer God answered. Instead, He sent people into our lives who loved the Lord and led us to a Christ centered maternity home and adoption agency.

We went to the adoption agency's orientation in March of 2001. We were to create a brief biography and picture profile of our lives. These profiles were given to prospective birth mothers who were considering placing their babies for adoption. In June, we received a call from the agency. They asked us to prayerfully consider a child who would be available within two weeks. It had been only a month before that my wife had been talking with the agency staff about the profile we had just submitted. They casually mentioned a young mother coming in for counsel. My wife secretly prayed and asked God if this was our birth mother.

You see, God worked this miracle to restore our souls. Our first daughter's birth mom gave birth to her in May. Originally she had planned to place the baby with friends of her family. Circumstances caused that plan to fail. Her grandmother, a strong Christian woman, suggested she call the adoption agency. We were not the first couple called. After much prayer, the first choice prospective couple decided this baby was not for them. Then we were called. We prayerfully considered. Ten days later, two days before Father's Day, we were blessed with a precious gift from God. She became our first daughter.

Her birth mom wanted to make sure she was placed before Father's Day. That wonderful act of love brought such special joy to our house. Our first daughter's birth mom chose us in part because she would be our first child, our princess. She wanted her daughter to have a close relationship with a father, something she did not have as she was growing up. Daughter number one is now seven years old, and not a Father's Day goes by that I do not feel awed in the miracle that God worked in our lives.

When our first daughter was fifteen months old, we decided to prepare a profile to try to adopt a brother or sister for her. We thought it might take some time before we were blessed again. We received another call just two months after we submitted the new profile. As we drove to our placement, we discussed names. We gave our second daughter a "musical" name. We hoped she would have a song in her heart. We had believed it was a miracle how we received our first daughter, and we believe that our second daughter came to us through the "grace" of God. "Grace" became our second daughter's middle name.

Our second daughter's birth mom chose us in part because we already had one adopted daughter. She also wanted her daughter to have a relationship with her father that she never had. She also wanted a big sister for her daughter so she would have something in common (adoption) and someone to share everything with. Our second daughter's birth mom prayed over us at the placement. Surely everyone could feel God's presence that day.

Those placements exemplify something I read in the maternity home's newsletter, "The birth of a child is an incredible gift of the Lord even when the choices that brought about the conception were less than perfect. Can you imagine the amount of selfless, sacrificial love a young woman must have as she seeks to restore her child back into the godly family design? Love for her child, combined with God's grace, gives her the courage to walk across the room and place her precious baby into the arms of a father she has chosen to guide her baby." I am overwhelmed when I read that passage and relive those placements.

When a child is adopted, there are some who call it being placed with their forever families. I like that. I like that because that's what I feel, knowing I've been adopted into the kingdom of faith, God's family. I've been placed with my forever family.

Fathers have a profound influence in their children's lives. I have often wondered what kind of father I'd be. My hope is that I can live up to the words we use to describe our birth mothers: Love that is selfless, sacrificial, courageous, and Godly. Knowing these young women is one of life's special blessings for me.

PROMISES IN THE RAINBOW

"I have set my rainbow in the clouds, and it will be the sign of the covenant between me and the earth." Genesis 9:13

Four days before we were to leave on our vacation, we got a call from our adoption agency's caseworker. She said a young woman was interested in us as adoptive parents. As you can imagine, we were excited and nervous at the same time. But this was not just any vacation, certainly not a vacation you could postpone at a moment's notice. A set of our good friends and we were going to Alaska. Quite a trip from Texas. We had a week booked at a beautiful lodge on the Kenai River. Our plans were to hike, kayak, sight-see, and fish for rainbow trout. After some discussion, the decision was made to go to Alaska.

Needless to say, the trip was wonderful, but our hearts were distracted with thoughts of a baby. Mid-week we were out for dinner and the manager of the restaurant approached our table asking our names. He told us we had a call at the register. Dumbfounded, I picked up the phone saying, "Hello." It was my best friend, Doe Doe. She had tracked us down, like the bloodhound she is, to tell us our caseworker had called. The birth mom was in labor.

The next day we decided to cancel our plans to go kayaking and to wait for news from Texas. We were so nervous and excited we could not sit still. To keep from climbing the walls, we had to get out of the room. My friend and I decided we would drive to Homer and do some shopping. Obviously, my husband didn't want to shop. He went to the lodge to get something to eat and to watch sports on television.

The drive to Homer was a beautiful coastal drive with lighthouses and picture- perfect scenery. It sure seemed long though. I remember our sitting in silence at times. Homer is a cool town on the bank of the Kachemak Bay in a sheltered arm of the lower Cook Inlet. It has a population of about 4,000 people. It is filled with artists and fishermen. Across the bay are snow-topped Kenai Mountains looking down on the cozy town as if to protect it.

This day, the day Rylee was born, I bought an original piece of artwork from an Alaskan woman. It depicted the scene I have just described above. I didn't know if Rylee was to be mine. If she were, I would give this piece of art to her some day. It would be a reminder of where I was and what I was doing the day she was born.

At the end of the day, my husband and I decided to indulge in the local cuisine before heading back to the lodge. On our way out the door, we passed a payphone and decided to call our caseworker. Standing in the lobby, on a payphone, I got the news. At 5:34 p.m. central standard time, Rylee made her entrance into the world: seven pounds, five ounces nineteen inches long, and absolutely beautiful.

I called my dad and Doe Doe. As we headed outside for the drive back to the lodge, there over the water, was a rainbow - not half of a rainbow, or even a small rainbow, but a big full rainbow was shining, as big as the sky itself. I could not believe it. I still did not know for sure if this baby would be my little girl. But God Himself reminded me, the promises of God are "Yea and Amen." I did not know what would happen, but I knew it would be great, and it is.

ALL DESIRES MET

**"Here am I and the children whom God has given me."
Hebrews 2:13b**

Several seemingly coincidental events in our lives kept bringing our thoughts back to China. By chance, my husband met a woman with two daughters adopted from China. These girls were drawn to him. He came home and mentioned we ought to think of adopting a girl from China. They have lost an entire generation of girls due to their one child policy. Many of the girls have been aborted, and the others were abandoned. I believe God heard the blood of these children crying out to him, and He raised up families to adopt because God is true to His Word. God values all life.

Additionally it has been my desire to have daughters. They were soft, gentle, quiet, mannerly, cuddly, and frankly manageable. China seemed like the logical source for a daughter.

First we would give medicine another try. Wouldn't a child we conceived be what God had for us? It *was* our desire. Doesn't God give us the desires of our hearts? With some medical intervention, we were able to have our first daughter, Annette. We still vaguely thought about adopting a baby girl from China. It was far in the back of our minds at this point. We had our daughter. Everything was perfect, except she needed a sister. We would try the same method that had worked the first time.

The next few years were very much like many other couples' experiences, full of medical procedures, painful, emotionally draining, hugely expensive, time consuming, and disappointing.

It was a particularly dark time for me. All through the Bible were stories of women who dealt with infertility. It was particularly devastating for women in that culture. It was no less devastating to me. Motherhood for women was an honor, a birthright, and an expectation. But, even in my low times, God was ever-present, refining me, refining our marriage, and refining our family. My husband was there, strong and steady, supporting

100

me through it all. We finally decided to discontinue the treatments and turn our hearts again to adoption.

Adoption gets a bad rap in our society. The news reports horror stories of birth parents returning for their children, and you hear of adopted children who had terrible problems. But according to the Bible, adoption has always been part of God's plan. The Egyptian princess adopted Moses. Then God used his heritage, as well as his environment, to prepare him for the leadership role for which he is remembered. There are others. Her Uncle Mordecai adopted Esther. Jesus was, in a sense, adopted by his earthly father, Joseph. The Bible describes how we, as Christians, are adopted by God into HIS family.

So, we started talking about adopting from China. I began making my plans. After going through the disappointment and loss of fertility, there was no way I wanted to worry about birth parents coming back to get the child. I wanted no surprises with someone showing up unexpectedly on my doorstep years down the road. Most importantly, I did not want anything to do with the birth mother. Additionally, I had watched my husband, who had been especially gifted by God to parent and develop a wonderful relationship with our daughter. I decided he was meant to parent girls. Besides, I had already observed that little boys were rough and tumble. They liked to climb on things and bring crawly creatures into the house. We just weren't used to that in our home.

So, it seemed that adopting a girl from China would be a perfect fit for us. When we started the process, we were told once we submitted all of the final paperwork, it would only be six months until we would receive our referral. The paperwork in an international adoption is brutal—literally several inches thick. It takes ages to go through all the requirements. They include a home study where the social worker visits your house several times and conducts interviews. We expected to receive word of our baby girl around February, 2006. We would be going to get her then. However, during the time we were working our way through the paperwork, China announced the time-frame for receiving a referral would be extended to a year and would continue to grow longer. Again, we were disappointed to receive the news that this process would be extended.

Interestingly, during this time, Todd started to mention he was concerned that people were not raising boys to become good men. He also lamented somewhat that he would never have a son. I listened and agreed. I knew there were great people who seemed to be handling the boy thing fine. I didn't really give it much thought. Let them raise the godly men.

Again, looking back, God was planting seeds. Things were moving along. We were in the waiting phase for China.

I met a co-worker who had adopted two children domestically. They had been unsuccessful in pursuing a China adoption. It was through this friend (who works at the Pregnancy Resource Center in our town) that we learned of a pregnant woman who was looking for a family to adopt her son. This new mom had not been able to locate, to her satisfaction, a couple for that adoption. My friend knew of our situation and called me.

The baby was a boy. There were no words to describe the emotion that surged through me that day. Was this a red herring? I managed to stammer out that I needed to talk with my husband, and I would get back to her. I decided this was not news to break to Todd over the phone. I needed to get to him in person.

I met Todd. After talking it over and digesting the information, we decided that yes, we would call back and say we were interested. When I called my friend, she was with the mom at the hospital because the mom had gone into labor. My friend suggested we come and meet her at the hospital. Todd couldn't get away from work right then. I drove erratically to the hospital. I took the elevator to labor and delivery, and stood outside the closed door. I was scared to go in. What if I did not like the birth mother? What if she did not like us? How awkward would this situation be? What if I broke down? As I think back, standing at that shut door, it is so symbolic of God providing the path for us. We still have to be willing to see the opportunity and take a step of faith. I believe God affords us these types of adventures often, but how many times do we choose to go through the door? Or do we stand there paralyzed with fear of the unknown that awaits us behind that door?

I eventually did step through the door, and Todd finally joined us. Between contractions, we got a glimpse of the mom, we were able to ask direct and specific questions of each other. At this point, the mom had not stated she would place the baby with us. But, throughout the process, I had the most incredible sense of peace. That is how I knew God was in control of the situation.

We received a phone call early the next morning. Turner was born around 3:30 a.m. We held him when he was only a few hours old. The mom told us then that she wanted to place Turner with us. We had no formal paperwork with this agency, so Turner went to the agency's foster care for a month while we completed another stack of papers. Turner was placed in our home one month later. This was a record time for an unplanned adoption. Eight months later, his adoption was finalized. God continued to be faithful. Looking back, God was also showing me He was in control.

There was an involved birth mother and birth father. It was a semi-open adoption, which meant we met and knew the birth mother. All of these things were what I had decided I did not want. Also, had our China adoption gone as originally planned, we would have been in China in February. We would have missed Turner.

After we got Turner, we began to wonder about going forward with China. Was this God's will? What should we do? Then one day God gave me the answer, "A double portion is laid up for you, Todd and Cindy." The seeds planted for China were all sprouting. Soon we were on our way to meet a beautiful China doll. We brought her home with us, and never looked back. Our hearts were too full with the three children God had divinely placed in our home.

Sometimes this question surfaces: "How can a mother give up her child?" Turner's birth mother was thirty-five and had a good job with benefits, but she was unmarried and knew she did not have the resources needed to give this child what he deserved. Her love for her son out-weighed her emotions and her circumstances. She was adamant that Turner have a mother and a father.

On the other hand, we know nothing about Emmy's mother or family. We do know she was living in poverty, in a culture that allows only one child per family. Her country has a social security system in which children take care of their parents. The people, whose entire identity stems from continuing the family name with sons, are pressured to choose only a son.

Our social worker described placing a child for adoption akin to the sacrifice Christ made on the cross for us. These mothers laid down their lives for their children. These mothers grieve for the children like they would grieve over a death.

My desire is to honor these mothers and fathers who valued life. I know God will honor their sacrifices. I cannot imagine a world without our three children. Each of these precious lives was part of God's greater plan. This has made motherhood so unique and special for me, in ways I never would have dreamed. There is no doubt in my mind that I was always meant to be their mother. I praise our Holy God whose plans for our lives are greater than we can ever imagine.

I lift up and honor our birth mothers who laid down their lives and provided for their children through the ultimate act of love. Motherhood is not just creating life. Motherhood is living out the act of love day-in and day-out.

TWIN BABY GIRLS

"He gives childless couples a family, gives them joy as the parents of children. Hallelujah!" Psalm 113:9 (The Message.)

It was not like me to take detailed notice of the physical world around me, but I was to see just how one phone call changed not only how I viewed nature but also how my husband and I were to grow from a couple into a family of four.

Early in the year 2008, things began to look differently to me. The groundhog in East Texas does not follow the rule. More than likely he will see his shadow on February 2. But even if six more weeks of winter were predicted, all our days were sunny. My husband and I had gotten a call in late January--a birth mother was considering an adoption placement plan for her children. She had chosen us!

The flowering trees looked more vibrant. The grass was greener. The breezes were gently warmer. Daffodils were smiling up at us everywhere we turned. Children playing in the parks seemed unusually carefree. Even the fluffy angel-like clouds directed our thanks heavenward, all because we had been selected as adoptive parents for a set of twins to be born in late March. We were thrilled!

We expected the twins to be placed soon after they were born on March 17. We *thought* we were ready. Our elation turned to dismay when complications arose concerning the birth dad.

Our education regarding the adoption process began to consume our lives. Before babies can be placed for adoption, the biological father must relinquish his parental rights as a part of the process. Two possible birth fathers were notified of the impending births. One man immediately relinquished his rights as the agency expected. The other man took everyone by surprise when he filed for custody. He then persisted with his case.

As the days became weeks and weeks became months, we wondered why things didn't move along more systematically and more quickly. We don't know how we survived the waiting. It seemed that there were so many "unknowns" as well as the fact that we could do nothing about them.

Thirty-six hours after their birth, the girls were discharged from the hospital and went to live with their temporary parents. They continued to live there for nearly four months. We, as prospective parents, continued to find solace during this wearisome process knowing that the babies were in good hands and were being deeply loved and cared for by their foster family. It was during these four months the foster couple taught us how to care for these newborn babies. We spent many days in their home on a regular basis in basic training for parenting. Eventually the girls began to sleep through the night and follow a regular routine 24/7. What a blessing for us, new parents of not one, but two babies.

Because we had developed a strong relationship with the foster family, we were aware of their grief when the girls left their home. They agreed letting the twins go after almost four months, was tough on their family. However, the smiles, the hugs, the softness, and those sweet baby scents more than compensated for the deprived sleep, colic cries, and the work involved in establishing a schedule. By the time the twins moved on to our home and family, we had made friends with their care-takers. But both of our families have continued to build on the relationship, and now we consider them part of our extended family.

We learned of the birth mom, initially, through a mutual friend who worked in the same organization we did. We were kept up to date more than usual concerning the birth mom because of the connection with our mutual friend. Our co-worker said the birth mother was quick to admit she had made some unwise choices in her life. But she had said the good, right choice (in spite of the pain, emptiness, and grief it caused her) was to choose adoption for the twins. She loved them and wanted for them what she could not provide. She knew the Lord would get her through it because she knew it was the right thing to do. The twins deserved a mom and a dad. She couldn't afford to hire a lawyer, nor did she want to fight the birth dad. She prayed if God led her to fight, it would not be *against* the birth dad but *for* the girls.

Our curious natures and our need to understand the entire adoption format kept us asking questions of everyone. We met with the agency weekly for progress reports and up dates.

At those meetings, we were told the following facts about the birth dad. He was in prison. He still wanted to exercise his right to be the father to these girls. He said his plan was to show up in court and give everyone hell, but after the first court hearing with no decision or conclusion, we were told, something began to happen inside him. He said his heart was changing. He asked God what he should do. Almost immediately, the guard came and introduced two visitors. The visitors were the adoption agency caseworkers. They answered his questions and explained away his misconceptions. They were not there to judge him or convince him to change his mind.

Before they left, the birth father indicated he might sign the papers--but not today. He wanted to talk with his mom first about the possibility of her taking the twins until he could get out of jail and prove he was capable of being a good dad. The workers prayed for him before they ended their visit.

Only a couple of days after that meeting, the birth father decided giving up his rights to parent was the right thing to do. He made his intentions known. The same two adoption workers went back to see him in the jail. The father confessed as he was processing his decision, he recalled how his growing up years with his mom had not been good. This was not the life he wanted for his daughters. Although his mom meant well, he realized theirs was a love/hate negative relationship. He said he was a changed man--even a new godly man. He signed the papers so the girls could be placed for adoption. The adoption workers gave him no pressure or judgment. They even prayed for him again before they left. The father's last words to them were, "Tell the girls I love them."

"And we know that all things work together for good to those who love God, to those who are the called according to His purpose." Romans 8:28

After four months of confusion, tears, uncertainty, and fighting, miraculously the biological dad and the birth mother both concluded parenting two babies would be more difficult than even the fight for custody had been. Each relinquished rights. We were overwhelmed at the reversal and the impact of the news--these twins could finally come home. It was a long, hard road. But we tell everyone it was worth every delay and every minute of the toil. We rejoice at what the Lord has done! And, He makes every day sunny.

IT'S A GOD THING

"Be anxious for nothing, but in everything by prayer
and supplication, with thanksgiving, let your requests
be made known to God; and the peace that surpasses all
understanding, will guard your hearts and minds through
Christ Jesus." Philipians 4:6-7

L ife is an exciting adventure. As such, it has its ups and downs.
My own mother worked around the church for over thirty years.
She had lots of folks praying for a grandchild for herself, and a child for
my wife and me. I remembered when we first took our daughter, Annie, to
daycare at the church. Everyone wanted to meet us. I quickly learned that
they weren't greeting me. It was Annie who was the attraction. One of the
ladies said, "Oh, this is Annie. We loved her before she was born."

I personally believe there is nothing more powerful than the prayers of
a mom, they become even more effective when friends join in agreement.

Our adoption story is like so many others. It began with hurt and
disappointment but ends in joy and happiness that can't be described.

We had tried to have children for many years. The anticipation from
month to month, only to be let down again and again, was taking its toll.
We were very happy with each other, but there seemed to be a piece missing
from our family. We decided to pursue adoption. To learn more about
adoption, we attended a few orientation sessions with various agencies.
Each proved to be a disappointment. None of them seemed "right." We
were discouraged . . . until God led us to a small Christian agency in our
state. Now it seemed God really cared about us. This agency had an annual
orientation for prospective adoptive couples, and as God would have it,
that event was scheduled just a few weeks away. We made plans, got our
paperwork in, and attended the orientation.

What a God-send it was! The workers had just the right words to
comfort and encourage everyone. These workers lived by faith and shared
tremendous testimonies. The entire process with them was based on prayer,
love, and ministry to these pregnant girls who were their priority. What a

great relief it was. Other agencies gave the feelings of pressure to work with them. We felt comfortable almost immediately with this licensed Christian agency. It was a ministry, not a business.

We had heard the stereotypical, negative stories about adoption, but during our visit with this group, we heard many positive, true stories. These were not the stories one hears on major media. They were not sensational enough to sell papers or to "increase" the number of listeners of the television or radio stations. These stories were just simple examples of how God had worked miracles in the lives of those in the adoption triangle. In one instance, a young girl spoke of choosing an adoption plan for her baby and of the placement experience. It was obvious how much of an unselfish act it had been. Her story was very different from what we had originally expected. Then two adoptive couples told their stories. It was so evident God had performed each miracle, and man could not have made it happen. We could not wait to get the process started. We determined to let God work in our lives and to let Him oversee each step of the way.

One of the ladies at the agency explained to us how the adoption process worked. We seemed to have an urgency in our spirits because we didn't want to miss out on the child God had for us. It felt as if once all the required steps had been done, the child would be ready for us. However, the hard part came when we had done everything, and then we had to "stand . . .and wait." So we waited and prayed.

When friends and family learned we were trying to adopt, we received several phone calls about possible private adoptions. As we talked with one of the agency workers, we were told that people who have waited many years for a baby will agree to almost anything to get that child. As hard as it was, we learned we must use good judgment when approached for a private adoption. We got a call from a girl who wanted to have her baby boy placed. We talked and even prayed. It all seemed fine. We even painted the baby's room a light blue. We picked out a name. We told our family and friends. Then two days before the baby was to be born, the girl called and said she had changed her mind. No warning, no explanation, nothing. We were heartbroken.

A few months later we received another call. It was a similar situation. We were determined not to let it happen again. We believed we had learned a hard lesson. We talked regularly to the girl and got to be friends. It seemed so right. This baby was a girl. We re-painted the baby's room. We picked out a girl's name. We waited for the birth. Guess what? It happened again. A few days before the birth, we received a message the girl had changed her mind. Heartbroken again, we became numb at this point. We had to call family and friends with the bad news. What was happening here? How could God do this? We cried out to God telling Him we would be good parents. We didn't understand. Had we fallen into that trap of wanting a baby so badly we would agree to anything?

A neighbor of ours had adopted, and she put things in perspective for us. She had gone through a similar situation. She said, "When you hold the baby in your arms, you will know instantly it was meant to be. You don't want someone else's baby. You just want the one God has picked out for you. It's a God thing." We began to realize we had put our desires in front of God's will. We had to begin to think God's way and to rise above our hurts. He knew best and had the right baby for us. Maybe she wasn't ready at the time we thought we were.

We had rushed through two preparations, which only resulted in the physical pain of grief. Now what? We had to do things the right way and not deprive God of His plan and His glory. We had to be patient and wait on God to work things out. Then just when we thought our call would never come, THE call came. The agency had a meeting set up with a potential birth mother in a few days. We were asked if we were interested. The clouds had parted and the sun was beginning to shine through.

We met the young lady and her family. We felt "peace that passes all understanding" in this situation almost immediately. We had lots in common and similar backgrounds. We felt like we had known one another all our lives. The young lady said she looked through a hundred profiles and pictures and none seemed right, but when she saw our scrapbook, she knew we were the couple for her baby girl. We also somehow knew this was God's plan. It just seemed so right. We had absolutely no control of the situation yet felt great peace about it. Though we are weak, God is strong. The young lady and her family felt the same way. The baby was due in three weeks.

Many people asked if we were nervous about *this* birthmother changing her mind. Not for one minute. Unbelievable as it seemed, we did not doubt for one second, even that early in the process. We knew, beyond a shadow of a doubt, this was the child our Heavenly Father had picked out for us. The birth mother had a healthy delivery. The baby was just perfect--her smell, her soft skin. Then we held her. A spiritual electric current went through our bodies! We knew she was our daughter. At that instant, all the hurt and anxiety we had felt over the years melted away. It disappeared and was replaced with great happiness and pride.

We tried to find words in the dictionary to describe how we felt about our birth mother. She had great courage and faith. She'll be in our prayers forever. We pray that someday, when the time and her situation are right, she has a houseful of children. God cares so much for His children, He puts those together in families whom He has chosen. He plucked people from all parts of the country and then put them together for a miracle-- plain and simple. It's beyond understanding.

We will be linked forever to the ladies at the agency, to our birth mother, and to her family. These are the folks for whom we pray daily. We witnessed a miracle first-hand. Our baby has brought us closer to God, to each other, and to tremendous happiness. Every day memories are made. This beautiful little girl reminds us of what matters in life. We had no idea we had so many friends who prayed for our family and how it was to be built.

Looking back, we see how God protected us in so many ways when we didn't even realize He was at work. Then He allowed us to be part of a life changing experience. The road was dark at times, but we learned never to quit. When we let God do the work, He proved Himself trustworthy. All the questions and all the answers can be summed up in one word: TRUST. It was worth the wait. Our adoption was, and continues to be, a "God thing."

GREG AND SHANNON

At Loving Alternative Adoption Agency it is rare to meet a couple who are open to adopting a child of any Race and any handicap. When a Black baby boy diagnosed with Sickle Cell, came to us from a birth mom at our maternity home, we called Greg and Shannon. We told them the entire story and asked them to pray about little Benjamin. Two things impressed me from the beginning about this couple. Shannon's first response to any situation in their lives was, "Let's pray." Greg was raised with the first and foremost rule in any situation being "obedience." Greg called his dad as they considered the situation. His dad said, "What does Jesus say about the 'least of these?'" Needless to say, Greg and Shannon adopted Benjamin.

During his first few weeks of life he lived in a godly temporary home. The foster mom prayed for and claimed Benjamin's healing. This young man is now four years old and thriving. Are prayer and obedience our first response in every situation that comes our way?

For the Love of Maddox

"For this child I prayed, and the LORD has granted me my petition which I asked of Him," I Samuel 1:27.

Our adoption journey began in our hearts after our second child was born with a rare, life-threatening genetic condition. We had always dreamed of having three children, but after her diagnosis, we realized there could be additional risks involved. We immediately turned our hearts to adoption, only to put it on hold, for a couple of years. We did find out the risk of having a second child with this same condition was very small, but the thought of adoption had already been planted in our hearts.

When our oldest was three and a half and our baby girl was almost two years old, we once again began to think about what we could do to expand our family. My sister-in-law was in the process of adopting a child from China, so naturally, we already knew adoption would be accepted in our family. We originally thought of adopting from Korea so we would have two Asian children in the family.

Within a month and a half, we were given the opportunity to attend a new couples' orientation through a small Christian adoption agency. The first night was amazing! We learned so much about adoption, the love of a birth mother, and the way this agency proceeds with adoptions. We also learned we were one of only a few of the couples at the orientation who were able to bear children. Our hearts broke as we heard their stories of infertility. We left that night in amazement of this adoption ministry, but with a sense of mourning for those wonderful couples who could not bear children. We almost decided not to go back to the second day of the orientation because of our daughter's birthday party, and the fact that the other couples there had no other option for building a family. We felt we were unworthy of proceeding with the adoption process. We did, however, want to learn more about the entire ministry and hoped to find ways we could be a blessing to them, other than through adoption. So, we arrived with open hearts on Saturday.

The executive director began to speak, and some of the first words out of her mouth were, "Some of you may be here and are able to bear children, and may even be feeling guilty about adopting because of these other families." She proceeded to tell us not to feel guilty, that God does not place babies in families strictly on the basis of infertility. He places babies in families He desires for them.

I stared at my husband and he nudged me. I said, "Can you believe she just said that?"

That was definitely the powerful work of the Holy Spirit. Had those specific words not come out of her mouth, we probably would not have proceeded. But now we felt so confident that I immediately began our scrapbook and biography. We had originally thought we could not handle a second boy, so we decided to ask the agency to present our profile only to birth moms of girls. For the first eight months or so we waited, and we heard nothing.

That entire fall, I kept hearing this still small voice saying, "Lindi, you have to open this up to what I have for you."

I kept those thoughts to myself and told the Lord if He thought so, He was going to have to convince my husband. I kept feeling the Holy Spirit nudging me, and I kept rejecting His commands.

One day in December, my husband leaned over to my four-year-old son and asked, "Mason, don't you want a baby BROTHER to ride four-wheelers with?"

My jaw dropped wide open and I asked, "What did you just say?"

We discussed what his suggestion was, and I knew it was God placing that desire in my husband's heart for a boy. Unfortunately, I was still apprehensive about calling the agency and telling them of our decision. I already had two difficult brothers and a wonderfully strong-willed son. The preconceived ideas I had about boys were simply from the few I had been exposed to in my home growing up, and as a mom. I had to begin to trust that God knew exactly what we needed. He would bring *our* child if I would just trust Him. So, I think it was January 10, 2006, when I finally got the courage to call.

On March 25th, we received a phone call that a birth mom had chosen us as the family she wanted to raise her son. Our emotions after that phone call were full of excitement, shock, disbelief, and humility that somebody would entrust such a precious treasure to our family. Maddox was born on January 17, 2006. I thank God every day that He saved him for us, and that He was gracious enough to keep him for us after my lack of obedience.

We had found out that Maddox's birth mom had intended to place him for adoption from the moment she found out she was pregnant. A few months before he was born, which was the time we were only open to adopting a girl, she had made the decision she would try to parent her child. At that time, she had not looked at any albums, and ours was not eligible for boy babies anyway. His birth was only a week after I called the office to open our profile to a boy. The week I had called, I felt such a burden lifted and an excitement for the son we could possibly have. Little did I know, that very week, our son would be born. Within a week or so of being home with him, our birth mother had called Fatherheart, the maternity home where she had lived during several of months of her pregnancy, to get help through their aftercare program. She displayed interest in placing her child for adoption. She really did want the best for this baby, out of love for him. When Maddox was a month and a half old, he entered foster care to allow this young mom the chance, prior to placement, to be sure she was making the right decision for her baby. She ended up taking him home over her spring break to say his good byes to the rest of the family. It was then she began looking over albums of families wishing to adopt. She chose our album. Without telling the birth dad, she gave him the albums she had in hand. He chose us as well. We received the phone call, and within a week, we had our precious baby boy. God had saved him for our family.

Within the first few days of having him, it was evident he was intended for our family. His personality was exactly what we needed. He was two and a half months old when he was placed with us. I missed the first couple of months of his life, but I am so thankful that God in His loving kindness, and our birth mom's sacrificial love, that together brought our son to us. The entire time we were waiting, I had prayed that our birth mom would love our child and would not make the decision to place him for adoption until she was definitely ready. (Having two other children, we had to consider the fact that their hearts could be broken if something fell through.) So I prayed this prayer, along with prayers of blessings for our child, everyday. I know for sure God answered my prayer by giving this young mom those first two months with him.

Adoption has changed our lives forever.

Meeting the birth couple was a very exciting and humbling experience. I had so many fears of being rejected by them, but God was in control the whole time and knew what He had in store. As his parents, we will always make sure Maddox knows the extent of love his birth parents had for him. The suffering of Maddox's birth parents at the placement ceremony was indescribable. The pain and hurt we felt for them was even greater than our pain when finding out our daughter had a life-altering, life-threatening condition.

There will always be a special bond of love between our family and theirs for the unselfish decision to place this precious baby boy into our family. Having given birth twice, I can say the love for our little man is no different than it ever was for our two children from my tummy. For anyone considering adoption, you'll find your lives will be forever changed, your hearts will be forever touched, and your family will be a witness to God's sacrificial love through adoption.

GOD'S MIRACLES IN OUR ADOPTION JOURNEY

"His unchanging plan has always been to adopt us into his own family by bringing us to himself through Jesus Christ. And this gave him great pleasure." Ephesians 1:5

As adoptive parents of four precious children, one facet of the story of Christ's birth always holds special meaning to us. Like our children, Jesus was adopted. He was the son of God, but His earthly father, Joseph, took Him as his own.

Every year we bake a birthday cake for Jesus, and I am reminded of the magnitude of God's love for us. He has used our children to illustrate that so well.

For you see, our children's birth mothers loved them sacrificially. In faith, they placed them into our arms, trusting that we would provide for their needs, raise them in a loving home, and teach them about Jesus. God, on the other hand, *knew* His precious son would be mistreated. He knew the very ones Jesus was sent to save would hang Him on a cross.

Yet He gave us Christmas. He gave us that magical night in the stable, shepherds, angels, and the glory of God in a squirmy newborn. Knowing all the ways we would fail Him, He adopted us into His own family--the family of God. And this gave Him great pleasure.

"He raises the poor from the dust and lifts the needy from the ash heap; he seats them with princes, with the princes of their people. He settles the barren woman in her home as a happy mother of children. Praise the Lord." Psalm 113:7-9

With four children, we have many, many miracles to tell! Some are obviously big and some may appear minor, but, when you put them all together, they testify to our loving God Who is working in even the smallest details of each adoption.

When we decided to stop trying to get pregnant and to apply for adoption, I was amazed at how free I felt. It forced me to take my hands off the situation and to truly wait for God's timing. We fully expected to wait one to two years, so when we were chosen after nine months we were shocked! My husband actually took the call, and I didn't believe him when he told me. It seemed surreal to think there was a baby boy growing inside a young girl who was going to allow him to become our son.

We met our son's birth mother two weeks before his birth. We were overwhelmed with love for her. I really didn't know what I would say when I saw her, but when she walked into the room, we both started crying and hugging each other. I could see so clearly how nervous and frightened she was. I wanted more than anything for her to know we would not only love this child, but we loved her and were committed to her.

After he was born, she changed her mind. Our social worker called to tell us. We were devastated, but honestly, we were not angry with her; we were heartbroken. We felt God had intended him to be our son, but we were not surprised she couldn't let him go after seeing his beautiful face. We called our friends and family and asked for prayer. We knew God could change hearts. We prayed for Him to change hers, but we did not expect it to happen.

That evening, our social worker called and said the birth mother had changed her mind again, and she had decided to place him in our home. God had, in fact, changed her heart. We could not believe it. We drove all night across the state and prayed constantly for her. It was so humbling to realize the huge price she was about to pay for her child.

Another miracle occurred during that time. We prayed for a fussy baby so the birth mother would not be left with a romantic or unrealistic view of parenting. Apparently that baby cried all night. Only sleeping on his birth mother's chest comforted him. The next night, his first with us, he barely made a peep. He was the quietest newborn one could have expected his first several days at home. God made sure we knew He had come through for us.

Our second child came to us fifteen months later--only six weeks after we had turned in our new album. Talk about a surprise. We expected, once again, to wait one to two years for our next baby; so, were we shocked when the agency called. This time our emotions were so different. We were in awe of what God was doing. We knew we were going to need His strength more than ever to have two babies fifteen months apart.

One week after we found out about our daughter, we met her sweet birth mother. She was a precious young woman who had had a very hard life. Because of her intense love for her baby, she wanted to give her a better life. She was very open with her grief. Our hearts broke for her because we could see how much she wished she could be the one to raise this baby girl. Once again, God gave us overwhelming love for our baby's birth mother. We committed to pray for her and to love her, regardless of her final decision. While we were there, her water broke (two weeks early). Our sweet baby girl was born just after midnight. Her birth mother stayed firm in her decision, and two days later, we met our daughter. We believe the fact that her birth mother was able to know her own limits and to love her baby enough to let her go was a huge miracle. How many babies end up in foster care because a mother tried but didn't realize her inability to parent until it was too late?

Our third child, another girl, was brought into our lives through much prayer and in need of God's intervention. Her birth mother, who was already raising a son, knew this baby needed to be placed for adoption. Not only was she unable to provide for her, her birth father would have been a very dangerous and negative influence in her life. This birth mom was truly modeling the example of Moses' mother by trying to ensure the safety of her child.

One week after we brought our tiny daughter home, we received a call that shook our entire family to the core. The birth dad wanted to fight the adoption. That meant, if the birth mother went ahead and relinquished her rights, the birth father would get custody of the baby. She was unwilling for that to happen, so she was forced to choose to parent, despite her desire for the baby to be where she felt God intended her to be—with us. We were terrified and immediately contacted friends and asked for prayer. We asked for three specific things.

1. That God would bring a godly man into her birth father's life to speak truth to him.
2. That God would not give him peace until he was obedient to God's will.
3. That her birth father would love her and want more for her than he could give.

God came through…completely. After five weeks of intense prayer and desperately loving this little girl, who may or may not become ours, we received the phone call we had been hoping for. God answered every single aspect of all three prayers, to the exact detail. We were amazed, thrilled, and in awe of the awesome and loving God we serve.

We believe there was another miracle. During all of this, it would have been so easy for her birth mother to have changed her mind, but she never wavered. She said that as much as she would love to raise this baby, she knew her daughter was where God wanted her to be. That was unbelievable clarity for a young woman who had just given birth and was in the throes of grief.

Seven months later, when her adoption was finalized, we cried as our hearts rejoiced over the fact that there we stood, before the judge, receiving the pronouncement that she was forever and irrevocably our daughter. When we shared the good news of God's miracle with our friends and family, these verses were especially meaningful.

"My grace is sufficient for you, for my power is made perfect in weakness" so that Christ's power may rest upon me. That is why, for Christ's sake, I delight in weaknesses, in hardships, in persecutions, in difficulties. For when I am weak, then I am strong." 2 Corinthians 12:9-10

A few weeks later, as we prepared to move out of state, her birth mother (in a letter) expressed a desire to see her one last time. We struggled with her request but we completely understood her desire. The fact was that she was still trying to get her own life together. The thought of watching her say "goodbye" to her daughter and start the grief process all over again seemed unwise and possibly harmful to her. How could we tell her "No"? God had it all under control. He performed another miracle. For three nights I had a dream, a very specific dream that was a letter I needed to write…dictated word for word by the Lord. I did not see Him, but I knew He was giving me the words. They were exactly the same for three nights. So, I wrote the letter and sent it to our agency. They sent it on to her. Later they told us it had been hard for her to read. She had cried, but it had seemed to mark a turning point in her grief. She had been able to let go and to begin to move on. It was a huge relief to know, without a doubt, we had done the right thing.

And then there were FOUR. Our sweet baby son was a surprise. We had just moved again and received the call that put us back on the adoption rollercoaster. We had thought our family was complete until we were told his birth mother was our oldest daughter's birth mother. Wow! Now that changed everything. Of course we would say, "Yes." God would have to come through to work it out, but we had to be obedient and available for whatever He was doing.

The situation was different this time. His birth mother was married to his birth father. Because of health and emotional problems caused by years of abuse, they knew they could not parent him. We felt so uneasy this time. Was it right to adopt a child from a married couple? Were they sure they couldn't do it? Maybe they just needed some help. Maybe we could help them. It didn't seem fair for them to have to do this. Oh, how we struggled. We prayed fervently for God's will. We had no expectations this time. We truly didn't see how they could release him. After all, they were married. So, we prayed that God would make it crystal clear to us what He wanted, and we committed to do whatever He asked.

Once again, He came through. When our son was born, they never wavered. They grieved. They cried. They cherished every minute they had with him, but they never wavered. We made the trip to pick him up with heavy hearts. It was such a sad situation. The day of his placement arrived, and Satan suddenly came out fighting. He tormented those precious birth parents. He tried to stop the adoption with guilt and lies from family members who did not approve of their decision. That was all the confirmation we needed. We got on our faces before the Lord and gave it up. Our hearts were in it. We realized this had become a rescue mission. If Satan was fighting it, then it must definitely be God's plan for this sweet baby to be our son. God came through. They tearfully, but freely, placed that precious baby boy in our arms. All we could do was look into his face with wonder. Another miracle. A gift beyond description. Lord, make us worthy of the trust they have placed in us.

We have, by the grace of God, been blessed with four children in six years. He is amazing! We gladly tell of the wonders God has done.

People often ask us if we were afraid of a birth mother changing her mind or of something going wrong. My response? Being a parent is risky no matter how you become one. All children are on loan to us from God. God builds families as He sees fit. We are blessed to be part of that process, whether through pregnancy or adoption. Parents lose children every day to miscarriage, disease, or tragedy. Avoiding the supposed "risks" of adoption in no way guarantees your heart will not be broken. Walking in obedience to God, though, guarantees being part of something bigger than yourself. We have the opportunity to witness Him at work. It is worth every minute of waiting, every tear, and every moment on your knees to receive a gift from the very heart of our Heavenly Father. "Perfect love casts out fear." I John 4:18 b.

I SING OF HIS LOVE

"Trust in the LORD with all your heart and lean not on your own understanding; in all your ways acknowledge him, and he will make your paths straight." Proverbs 3:5-6.

"I will sing of the mercies of the LORD forever. With my mouth will I make known your faithfulness to all generations." Psalm 89:1

"I could sing of your love forever . . . I could sing of Your love forever." These lyrics dance through my head as I look at my precious child sitting in her car seat. With a big smile on my face, I say to myself, "YES! I can sing of Your Love, God! You have blessed me so immensely!" Those words are so incredibly true, and our adoption story is an example of His enduring love for us.

In March of 2005, we had finally made the decision to adopt, and we started the process with an agency in Texas. With anxious hearts, we began preparing our profile. God would use something in our life book to connect us with one very special birth mom. The book was completed and sent to the adoption office in July. We thought to ourselves, "Yeah!!! We're officially expecting!"

Out of our anxiety and the need to keep this journey in our control, I thought of an excuse to call the agency for an up date. In reality my call would be a reminder to them of who we are. We were here, ready and waiting for that baby we would get from them. So I called.

As it turned out, my call was timely. Isn't it just like God? Our agency's caseworker revealed to me we had been chosen by one of the young women at their maternity home. The agency hadn't called us yet as this had the possibility of a different end result from the mom's desire. The birth dad had said he would fight the adoption. Legally both birth parents' rights have to be terminated. She would parent her child rather than allow the birth dad to have automatic custody. The agency wanted to protect our emotions until things were settled. Too late. We became emotionally immersed. In the dilemma, and prayers, we felt God say, "Trust Me."

We have all heard stories of how an adopted child was returned to birth parents months, or even years, later. This can happen in real life, but our agency does all that they can to terminate the birth dad's as well as the birth mom's, parental rights prior to placement. In Texas, if a birth dad doesn't voluntarily waive his rights, he is served a citation. He has twenty-one days to file a reply. He can choose to sign the papers, ignore them, or hire a lawyer and fight the adoption. If he ignores the papers and the twenty-one days pass, he will lose his rights by default. If he chooses to hire a lawyer, a court will decide the case.

This particular birth dad was served. Twenty-one days crawled by with no word. Each day that we didn't hear he had responded gave us encouragement. Surely he would not fight the adoption if he hadn't done so by now.

We were also encouraged when the agency workers invited us to meet the birth mom and her family.

Meeting them all, and falling in love with every one of them, took our already stretched emotions to a whole new depth. God continued to test our obedience to His "TRUST ME."

Our birth mom had been adopted into her family as a child. During the several weeks of uncertainty with the birth dad, the baby's grandmother cared for this (our) child. This woman knew first-hand what it was like to dream of a child and not conceive. Almost twenty years ago, the Lord had put a baby into her arms. Now she would take care of someone else's baby for several weeks. The heart-breaking thought must have gone through her mind constantly, "I will be placing this child into the arms of a waiting adoptive couple. Can I do that?"

God's words, "Trust Me" kept me from giving up. Throughout this time, I was reminded of Abraham and Isaac. I thought about how God had told Abraham to sacrifice Isaac. Abraham was such a faithful servant, he did exactly what God told him to do, and he didn't know what was going to happen. He trusted the Lord. Just like Abraham, we didn't know what was going to happen with the baby. All we had to do was listen to Him and to trust in Him. How hard was that? Extremely hard! It sounded easy enough intellectually, but emotionally, it was humanly impossible.

As it turned out, the birth dad did answer the summons. Three court sessions later, and our fingernails chewed to knuckle length, the birth dad stated he really did not believe he was the one to have full custody of this child. He signed his waiver of interest. This baby was ours!

As they say "The rest is history." Just as God kept His promise to us as we trusted Him, He has also worked to heal the birth family of their time of grief.

She's a delightful little girl. She's always happy and smiling. In fact, I think a better word to describe her is "joyful." I think back to a time when I thought I knew what was best in my life, and I that's what I wanted, not thinking of *God's* best. He really does want to give us our hearts' desires; we just have to learn to ask and to trust that He will provide in His perfect time. I can sing of His love forever, and I will.

APPENDIX

A NOTE FROM ME TO YOU

I think about you often.
And I'd write you every day.
But there seems so very little
That seems worth while to say.

It either rains or doesn't
It's either hot or cold.
The news is all uninteresting
Or else it's all been told.

The only thing that matters
Is the fact that you are there
And I am here without you
And it's lonesome everywhere.

I think about the way you smile,
And I recall your touch.
And tears come all the while,
And I miss you very much.

written by Amanda E. Shaw
1895 after the death of one of her sons.
1896 (Doris Howe's grandmother)

Dear Precious Michael

I love you dearly
with all my heart.
But I am truly sorry
We had to part.

God gave you to me
And I gave you to another
That's all I think about
From day to day.

Trusting in God
I can cope.
I pray to our Lord
And I don't give up hope.

I would have kept you
But it would have been sad
To see my son
Grow up without his dad.

You have Bill and Sandy
Who love you so much.
They'll prove it to you
With every gentle touch.

Love your Mother and Father.
They'll show you the way.
My prayers will be with you
Each and every day.

When you're feeling
In doubt about my Love
Get on your knees
And pray to our God above.

With Love,
Tamala

FOR ELLIE
FROM ELIZABETH

It's not that I can't live without you,
It's that I don't even want to try.
Every night I dream about you,
How will I ever say goodbye?

Every second we get closer
To the day when you will go...
Turn your back and walk away -
Who knows where you'll go?

Promise me you'll look back,
And keep me in your heart.
For if you always do this,
We will never be apart.

So, if we never meet again
Along life's painful journey,
Simply remember this;
You are always loved, and very truly missed.

Love, Elizabeth

FROM MY HEART

A birth mom's mother wrote these notes, emptying her heart before several hundred folks at an annual banquet.

"The strength of what you believe is measured by how much you're willing to suffer for it."

I didn't know when I wrote that phrase down many years ago just how much I would come to understand what it meant.

March 31, 1999, was the end of my life as I knew it, and the beginning of another.

April 1, began at 1:00 a.m. for me. The night was broken by the jangle of the phone. My daughter, crying, was trying to tell me she thought she might be pregnant. The desperation in her voice paralleled the destruction of my heart. (Ninety-five percent of what you fear never happens, but they don't tell you what to do if it does.)

My husband and I raced to where she was. It was a living nightmare--no matter how fast we drove, it seemed to take forever to get to her. We stopped at a 24-hour pharmacy and got a pregnancy test. She took it as soon as we got her home. There they were, two pink stripes. After finding out some of the information about how this could have happened, we decided there was nothing we could do until morning. So I crawled into bed next to my sobbing daughter. As I tried to calm her, all I could think of was "Who is this child?" Usually I try to find humor in the midst of horror, but let me tell you, there is nothing funny about an unplanned crisis pregnancy. The range of emotions began with tears.

I cried at the doctor's office when they told me their test had also read positive and we needed to see an OB.

I cried at the OB doctor's office as we entered the waiting room and saw all the smiling faces of the soon-to-be moms, who, at the right time, were celebrating life, as we were suffering the loss of innocence.

I cried at the intimate questions they asked, the tests they said MUST be done (such as Hepatitis, the other STD's, and AIDS.)

I cried when the doctor let us listen to the heartbeat, because up until then, I just knew she was going to tell us it had all been a mistake. It was a virus or a hormone imbalance.

I cried in my pastor's office as we discussed how and when to tell our church family. You see, this happens to other people but not to those who raise their children in the church, sing on the praise team, work in the youth group, and obey God.

I cried every time I had to tell someone and saw the pain move across their faces for us.

The crying was just the beginning of the range of emotions I felt as a mother.

I felt intense sadness when I thought of how my daughter had thrown away the best part of life, her high school years of sports, proms, pep rallies, puppy loves, and sleep-overs with her friends, for one night of stupidity.

I was angry because I was having to suffer the consequences of her actions right along with her, and I had done nothing wrong!

I grieved the broken trust and wondered if I would ever be able to have a right relationship with her again or even worse, if I would want one.

I felt such shame every time I had to look at someone and wonder what they knew or had heard, or if they even knew anything at all. Should I tell them? How much should I tell? Did they have a right to know?

The grief and sorrow that rippled through my life was like a stone that had been cast into the water, especially after we'd decided adoption was the option God wanted us to choose. My daughter would not raise her first child, and I would not be a grandmother to my first grandchild.

GOD FELT EVERY EMOTION I FELT.

How sad He is when His creatures fall.

How great was His anger when Satan had taken from Him that intimate loving relationship He had with His childen in the garden. It would never be the same.

Broken trust: He had trusted them with everything, and they had had perfect freedom in the garden.

Imagine the grief He felt when He decided that in order to restore us, He would have to sacrifice His own beloved Son.

How bittersweet must have been the sorrow He felt as He watched Jesus become flesh and dwell among us, knowing He would suffer and die at the hands of the very ones He had come to save.

Oh, the shame God felt when Christ took upon Himself the sins of the whole world. Our Holy Father was so filled with shame, He had to turn His face away.

We experience these emotions and weep for ourselves, but try to enlarge them through the magnifying glass of Holiness! Every time one of us sins, even the slightest, our Holy God intensely feels these emotions over and over again. Now multiply that pain by the number of people living today. When we allow ourselves to think about this, His love becomes bigger, His provision more precious, His grace more sufficient, and His plan more miraculous!

We heard about the maternity home from my sister. After receiving information from them, we knew this was where God was going to work. It was a bitter sweet reality. Once again, I was pulled by emotion. On one hand, I wanted to be the one who stood beside her and guided her through this, step by agonizing step, because I was her mother. That's what mothers do. But at the same time, I was so hurt and angry and confused, I wasn't sure I would be able to do it. She, on the other hand, needed to be in a place where there were no distractions and she could hear from God. She needed a place where people could help her objectively but empathetically. She needed to be with people she could relate to, who knew what it was like to be sixteen and pregnant. It was yet another of the difficult decisions we would have to make, but it was one of the best. Believe it or not, when people would ask us what we were gong to do, and we told them, the response we most often received was "Why are you sending her away? Are you punishing her?" Knowing they had no clue, I would reply, "My goodness, NO, we are sending her there in order to save her."

I will never forget the day we had to drive her over there. Again, it was a tearing of my heart. It was the only time in my life I can remember praying our car would break down in the middle of nowhere and no one would help us. We would have to just stay there on the side of the road forever. I can't find words for the anguish I felt as we left her there. Those first days were rough and full of phone calls, but ever so gradually, we began to experience more and more "God moments."

I volunteer at our local crisis pregnancy center, and whenever a girl wants to know more about adoption, I am the one she sees. Through our story, I am able to minister to her and refer her to a maternity home where Love and God reside, to tell her first-hand how God uses that place to heal, to restore and to save lives. Whether God calls a girl to make an adoption plan or to parent, He uses this ministry to prepare her.

It has been ten years since that placement. While the pain has lessened, it still tries to rise up from time to time, but that's okay because that is when I let God hold me. Sometimes, it is in the form of a question, like, "Why?" and He says to me, "You don't need to know *why* you just need to know *that* I knew, and I planned it this way." So, we choose to accept it and embrace it and take joy in it, and He chooses to bless us for our obedience.

Our daughter is so much more than she ever would have been had she not seen God in all His glory. She has graduated from college with a 3.7 G.P.A. She was blessed with a scholarship from a famous foundation. That scholarship also made it possible for her to do inner-city missions work in a distant city during a summer program. She has a heart for the Lord that is evidenced by her life, her words, and her walk. She is His child, she is my daughter, and she is my best friend.

Eventually, God took all our pain and began to reveal His glory to us. He provided everything we needed, and one of those things was the ministry at the maternity home. It was there that He began the restoration of all that had been broken. It was through that ministry that He brought together, forever, two families whom He had prepared "before the foundations of the earth," (each with his own need) to complete His plan. He revealed His perfect will and set all of us on a new course.

It was through this trial that I was able to live the words of Paul in Romans 5:3-4.

"We can rejoice, too, when we run into problems and trials, for we know that they are good for us--they help us learn to endure. And endurance develops strength of character in us, and character strengthens our confident expectation of salvation."

"For you have been given not only the privilege of trusting in Christ, but also the privilege of suffering for him." Philippians 1:29

Be willing to suffer for what you believe because it is in the suffering that we see God at His greatest. It was in that suffering that I heard my call. And it is from that suffering I am able to serve Him. In Genesis 50:20, Joseph spoke these words to his brothers: "Do not be afraid, for am I not in God's place? You meant this for evil, but God meant it for good, so that many lives would be saved." God has put us in His place, and as we continue to share our story and to support this ministry, He continues to save lives. Satan loses and our God reigns.

This is a partial list of those who have helped to make this collection of stories possible:

Carolyn Hammond
Darlene Ryan
Kathleen McLarnon
Wendy Lanier
Grace and Dennis
Duane and Amy
Troy and Melissa
Monte and Toni
Mike and Jessica
Ross and Staci
Jim and Pamie
Kyle and Jeanine
Tim and Pam
Brian and Warrie
Bob and Laura
Tim and Trena
Joyce and Junior
Mark and Amanda
Daniel and Lindi
Greg and Shannon
Terry and Lindsey
Marty and Daina
Bandon and Lisa
Gregory and Robin
Joe and Michelle
Mike and Kim
Jay and Christine
Peter and Patrice
Wes and Sue
Don and Darlene
Harold and Ceceila
Jim and Christy
Todd and Cindy

ADDRESSING THE MARKET

Adoption Joys targets:

First: Prospective adoptive couples: "God still does miracles. What He's done for others He can do for us."

Second: Adoptive couples: "These stories are reminders of the miracles God performed in our family to bring us these children."

Third: Birth families: "When I learned how adoptive couples are trained to send pictures and letters, as well as to pray for me and to love me for years to come, I saw adoption as a positive option so different from what I thought I knew before my decision. They love me not just my baby. I made the adoption decision out of our love for my baby."

Fourth: Adoptee: "I have a loving birth family and a loving adoptive family. I'm doubly loved."

Fifth: General public: "These positive stories are real. They are unlike the negative ones we see on TV or read about in the papers."

Sixth: Thousands of post abortive women: "I had no idea this was option for me during my unplanned pregnancy. I might have chosen adoption."

ADOPTION:
A loving embrace,
a miraculous joining of souls,
a gift of God,
a reflection of Heaven.

In our fallen world, with promiscuity high, abortions rampant, and dangerous additives in our fast foods causing infertility, adoption as a topic is becoming a household word. I believe ***Adoption Joys/ They Expected a Miracle***, will bring a ray of hope to the three principals in the adoption journey. Through the book, God's miracle work will be glorified helping the faith of many to grow in Him.

LaVergne, TN USA
15 March 2011
220256LV00002B/2/P

9 781449 712921